D1450581

THE FINE PRINT
OF SELF-PUBLISHING

THE CONTRACTS & SERVICES OF 48 MAJOR SELF-PUBLISHING COMPANIES
— ANALYZED, RANKED & EXPOSED

MARK LEVINE

THE FINE PRINT OF SELF-PUBLISHING: THE CONTRACTS & SERVICES OF 48 MAJOR SELF-PUBLISHING COMPANIES — ANALYZED, RANKED & EXPOSED

PUBLISHED AS A JOINT VENTURE BY BRIDGEWAY BOOKS AND BASCOM HILL PUBLISHING GROUP
212 3RD AVE. NO., SUITE 471
MINNEAPOLIS, MN 55401

For more information about this book contact 612-455-2290, ext. 201 or visit www.book-publishers-compared.com

Library of Congress Control Number: 2006923682

ISBN-10: 1-933538-56-2
ISBN-13: 978-1-933538-56-3

TABLE OF CONTENTS

INTRODUCTION

For most authors, writing is a part of who we are—our thoughts and ideas constantly percolate as dialogue and plot twists in our minds. Kurt Vonnegut summed it up best when he said, "Most people do other things with their time. But writers, we'll sit around and think up neat stuff, not something just anyone could do."

Writing a book is an amazing accomplishment. When I finished my first manuscript, I felt the way a runner feels after completing a marathon for the first time.

But if publishing your manuscript and turning it into a book is your goal, then finishing the manuscript is just the beginning.

Until the mid-1990s, there existed three ways to become a published author:

1. Submit a manuscript to agents and traditional publishers, such as Random House or Dell Publishing, and hope you were one of the chosen few
2. Pay a vanity publisher $10,000 to $20,000 to print your book, which got it "published" but left you deep behind the financial eight ball before you sold one book
3. Or utilize self-publishing, which required you to handle all aspects of book publishing, including finding a printer and cover design, formatting, obtaining an International Standard Book Number (ISBN) and UPC Bar Code, and locating sales and distribution avenues.

Over the past five to seven years, however, new production technologies and the Internet have spawned a new industry segment. Electronic publishing (epublishing) and print-on-demand (POD) publishing give writers more opportunities to become published authors.

POD publishers (PODs) allow a book publisher or printer to produce the number of books actually ordered. These publishers are hybrids of traditional publishers, vanity presses, and self-publishing companies. Several publishers reviewed in this book have complained about being labeled as PODs. They argue that POD is merely a method of production and limited distribution, and should not be confused with self-publishing, which uses the author's financial resources to publish a book. That is true. However, I suspect that these publishers disdain association with the term mostly because several scummy publishers have dirtied the word, and given these publishers an undeserved black mark.

Well, friends, in this book, I call them PODs because (1) many laymen outside the publishing world continue to refer to these publishers as PODs, (2) this book is long, and abbreviations like this make it easy for you to read, and (3) I'm trying to keep this book affordable and every extra page adds to its cost. So, for you publishers reading this now, relax, no one who reads this book is going to come away thinking that POD means anything nefarious.

The Fine Print of Self-Publishing only covers royalty-paying PODs (the extended ebook version of the book includes some PODs not large enough to make it in here and many epublishers that strictly publish electronic books). Most PODs now charge up-front fees. Some have wider distribution channels than others. And like traditional publishers, some are selective in what they will publish while others publish anything so long as the writer pays the publishing fee.

All publishers featured in this book have these common characteristics:

- Accept submissions from new or inexperienced writers without requiring the writer to have an agent.
- Publish the book in six months or less (in most cases 30 to 90 days).
- Don't pay an advance.
- Offer little or no marketing budget for the author's book, but sometimes provide these services for a fee.
- Pay higher royalties than traditional publishers.
- Charge up-front publishing fees.

CHAPTER 1

Don't Wait Any Longer To Publish
Your Book—Make Your Own Big Break

Whether your idea of a big break is to have your book published so your story can be read by family and friends or to become the next A-list writer on the best seller lists, you have some decisions to make.

You can polish your query-letter-writing skills and spend the time it takes to get your manuscript into the hands of an agent or traditional publisher. You can also attend writers' conferences to network with agents and publishing executives. Regardless of your talent, the odds are stacked against you.

Still, you can become the next J.K. Rowling and be a hero to writers everywhere!

If you're reading this book you've probably experienced the get-an-agent-and-find-a-publisher circuit without much luck. Yeah, it would be awesome to tell your friends that Random House just signed you. But even if that happened, you'd still be a small fish in an ocean and worse off than if you'd published your book through one of the PODs discussed in this book. Forget the agents and the publishers—you don't need them.

How can that be? Simple.

If Random House publishes Joe Nobody's book, it probably won't dump a bunch of money into marketing. If Joe's lucky, he'll get $5,000 to $10,000 in marketing efforts from the publisher. But Joe still has to do all the real marketing on his own. And if the book takes off through Joe's efforts, Random House takes all the credit and Joe only makes a five percent royalty. The only benefit to him is that Random House foots the bill for costs such as printing, editing, and cover design.

If you don't have time or don't want to handle the aspects of pure self-publishing, there are plenty of excellent PODs who can ready your book for readers. Persuading readers to buy your book through Amazon.com or the publisher's web site is up to you. For between $500 and $6,500, you can have your book ready to sell. Yes, you paid the up-front costs of design and layout, but you own the book outright, and your royalties will amount to at least four times more than Joe Nobody's contract with Random House would have paid. Plus, if you act on the tips in my book, and your book takes off through your marketing efforts, you can pull it from the POD publisher, self-publish and keep 100% of the royalties or shop it around to agents and traditional publishers.

Once you've sold several thousand copies and proven your marketing ability, Publisher X and Agent Y, who rejected your book one year ago, will now do anything to get their hands on it. Publishing your book with one of the recommended publishers in this book is by no means a second-class way to become a published author. It is an opportunity to make your book available, garner the attention you deserve, and tell your story. If you are a talented writer, readers, agents, and big-time publishers will find you.

It took me six years to become proactive about publishing my first novel, *I Will Faithfully Execute*, through a small publisher that later became a POD publisher. In 1994, when I finished the novel, I put it into the hands of a few big-time publishing houses. They all told me the same thing, "We like the writing, but in order for us to sell it you have to rewrite this and rewrite that, then send it back to us." I wasn't about to start rewriting my book so that maybe some traditional publisher would take it. I didn't have the time because my law practice took off and demanded much of my energy. My manuscript languished in my computer's hard drive for six more years.

In 2000, when I founded Click&Copyright (www.clickandcopyright.com), an online copyright registration service, I discovered a whole world of self-publishing companies.

Because I believed the self-publishing route was a waste of time, I only submitted my manuscript to publishers who accepted e-mail submissions. I ignored any publisher that required a hard copy submission or query letter. To my surprise, I received several offers. I ultimately chose Bookbooters Press because they charged no publishing fees, offered free editing services, paid decent royalties, agreed to a non-exclusive contract, and expressed genuine interest in my manuscript. Today, these favorable terms are virtually unavailable. No POD publisher that I know of offers free publishing, editing, cover design, and more.

I Will Faithfully Execute was named Bookbooters Book of the Year for 2000–2001, and has remained on its best seller list for much of the past five or more years. The novel is a political thriller that takes place inside a presidential campaign. In fact, it was one of the first books former President Clinton read when he left office.

My experience with Bookbooters made it easier to attract agents and publishers to my second novel, *Saturn Return*, a novel of kismet and self-discovery, and several screenplays (the screenplay I wrote based on *Saturn Return* was a semi-finalist in the Chesterfield Screenplay Competition in 2000).

Had I not published with Bookbooters, I would probably still be waiting for something to happen with my book. I made it happen for me. If you do it right, you can also make it happen for you.

Let's talk about how *The Fine Print of Self-Publishing* and my years of experience as a lawyer and author can benefit you and improve your publishing experience.

The rest of this book explains:

- What to look for when choosing a POD publisher
- What POD contracts really say and how to negotiate better terms with a publisher

- How to ensure you receive the best deal
- The differences between 75 of the biggest self-publishing companies

I tell it like it is. I'll tell you when a publisher's contract is so bad that you'd have to be insane to sign it. I'll also tell you when a publisher offers an exceptionally favorable contract and service.

I have no allegiance to any publisher covered in this book. In researching this book, I uncovered unfriendly terms in several publishers' contracts. Several of the companies I rate highest (iUniverse, BookPros, Xulon, Cold Tree Press, and Wasteland Press) willingly removed language that was not author-friendly. My only allegiance is to you, the author.

As you can imagine, I hear horror stories from writers all the time, some of which are included in this book. If you choose one of the good publishers featured in this book and follow the tips in this book, you can avoid these horror stories. I can't promise stupendous book sales or even modest profits. What I can promise you is that you won't get scammed and fleeced.

CHAPTER 2

Why You Need To Read This Book

If you decided to buy a television or a car, you might read *Consumer Reports* to find the best price and highest quality. Spending hard-earned money to publish your book should be approached with the same careful attitude. Self-publishing companies are not in business to make you a successful author. They are in business to make money by selling products and services to you. I'm in the business of helping authors find and choose a publisher that offers a superior product at a fair price.

Here are a few reasons why you need to read this book:

- To know what you need to look and watch out for when choosing a POD publisher.
- To understand all the legal gobbledy-gook in the publishers' contracts.
- To save money and negotiate the highest percentage of royalties.

Through my involvement with Click&Copyright and my moderator role in copyright law discussions for various online writing schools and organizations, I met many writers who were involved in contractual disputes with PODs. In fact, several writers hired me to get them out of their legal jams.

My experiences with these cases made me realize the need for this book. All of my clients' problems with the publishing contracts could have been avoided if they had understood the publishing agreements when they first signed them. Yes, some of my author-clients who were told one thing were then slipped a contract that said something else. Had they carefully read the agreement and understood what specific sections within them meant, they might have avoided their publishing nightmares. This book explains what these contract clauses mean and helps you spot unscrupulous ones.

If you were signing a contract with Random House, you'd hire a lawyer, right? But when you sign with POD Publisher XYZ, your legal fees could exceed all the money you hope to make from the sales of your book. That's why I wrote *The Fine Print of Self-Publishing*: to help writers understand POD contracts and enable them to find the best publishing situations which fit their goals and expectations.

I can't give you legal advice, but what I can do is use my legal training, knowledge, and experience to show you what POD contracts really say and which publishers provide the best service for the best price.

I can promise you that if you follow the advice in this book you won't get ripped off by any self-publishing company and may, in fact, negotiate a better deal. If you don't follow the advice here you may find yourself spending thousands of dollars in legal fees to battle an unscrupulous publisher.

CHAPTER 3

The Nine Qualities of a
Good Self-Publishing Company

Every worthy self-publishing company has the nine qualities listed below. If you're already considering a specific publisher, go through this list of qualities and make sure it matches up with your publisher. If the publisher you're considering doesn't have most of these qualities, you'd be better off finding a different publisher.

1. Good reputation among writers (I show you how to obtain private-eye information about a prospective publisher)
2. Attractive, easy-to-navigate web site
3. Fairly priced publishing fees
4. Generous royalties without any fuzzy math
5. Low printing costs and high production value
6. Favorable contract terms
7. Fairly priced additional services (such as marketing and copyright registration)
8. Ability to obtain an ISBN, UPC Bar Code, and LCCN (Library of Congress Control Number) as part of any basic publishing package
9. Ability to register the author's book with Bowker's Books In Print, make it available through a book distributor like Baker & Taylor or Ingram, and list it on Amazon.com, BarnesandNoble.com, and other large-scale sellers

1. Good Reputation Among Writers

Learn what your peers are saying, especially those who have published with the publisher you're considering. Most publishers include testimonials on their web site from "satisfied" authors—these are sugarcoated and even if they were true, I'd still dig further.

Don't ask the publisher for authors you can contact—you'll only get the happy ones. Instead, go through the web site and pick out five authors to contact. Most publishers have a page on their web site for each author with the author's contact information. E-mail the authors and ask them about their experience with the publisher and whether they're satisfied with the publisher's level of services.

Don't stop there. Put your ear to the ground. There are web sites that do the sleuthing for you and provide warnings about shady publishers.

Try these:

- Google Groups (http://groups.google.com/). This is my personal favorite. Just type in the name of the publisher, and you'll get links to each posting where someone has discussed them.
- Writer Beware (www.sfwa.org/beware). If a publisher is criticized here, stay away.
- Writers Weekly Warnings (http://www.writersweekly. com/whispers_and_warnings.php). Another credible web site for the truth about publishers.
- Preditors & Editors (http://www.anotherealm.com/prededitors). This web site tells it like it is. The web site also has links to scores of other web sites that contain warnings about publishing scams (http://www.anotherealm.com/ prededitors/pubwarn.htm).
- Absolute Write Water Cooler, Bewares and Background Checks (http://absolutewrite.com/forums).

2. Attractive, Easy-To-Navigate Web site

If a publisher's web site is dingy, cheap-looking or hard to maneuver, what kind of presentation do you think your book will have? Even if potential readers can find the web site, they will be less inclined to purchase a book from a cheap-looking web site because they'll question the publisher's credibility, secure ordering system, and more.

Just like in the off-line world, a professional image means a lot.

Go through the publisher's web site and see if you can find any place where it notes the last time the web site was updated. Any business that has an active online component constantly up-dates and tweaks its web site. If a publisher hasn't updated its web site in more than 12 months, it means it probably isn't paying much attention to its customers or authors.

In an earlier version of this book, I focused a lot on a pub-lisher's internet traffic. Keep in mind that such traffic isn't may not reflect traffic of potential book buyers. Yes, many PODs spend tens of thousands of dollars to drive traffic to their web sites, but the traffic they want is potential authors. So, tons of traffic won't necessarily benefit you.

It still is useful to see where all the publishers rank as far as traffic. I used to rate and compare the traffic for all the publishers covered in this book using Alexa's ranking. Alexa is a site that ranks the traffic to a website and is based on factors such as incoming links and other analytics. Alexa rankings aren't the gospel and are included in this book only as a guide. An Alexa ranking of 200,000 or less is pretty good.

3. Fairly Priced Publishing Fees

Choosing a publisher involves more than price comparisons. The fees for print-on-demand are all over the board and are based on many factors. Depending on the services provided, the price of what is fair ranges from $200 to $6,500. Three of the best self-publishing companies have publishing fees from $217 (Booklocker.com) to $750 (InfinityPublishing.com) to $6,500 (BookPros.com). Each offers services that made me rank them as one of the outstanding self-publishing companies. Will the physical quality of your book be better for $6,500 than for $200? Of course, but that isn't always the sole consideration.

No matter what package you choose from any publisher, a quality publishing package should include:

- High quality, custom-designed book cover (Don't use a template offered by any publisher—covers sell books)
- Professional layout of the book
- Registration with Amazon.com, BarnesandNoble.com, and other online retailers
- A page on the publisher's web site (unless the publisher doesn't sell books through its web site)
- The ability to purchase your own books for a reasonable price
- A contract that you can cancel anytime

If you're serious about your book, you will need to have it edited, not by a friend or your old English teacher, but by a real editor. Many publishers provide this service for an additional fee, so if you haven't done so already you need to consider this service (one reason BookPros' initial fee is so high is because it provides complete editing). Editing costs should be around $.01 per word for standard copy editing (spelling, grammar, punctuation) and $.02–$.03 per word for more substantive editing. Most self-publishing companies charge more than $.01 per word for standard copy editing. To combat that, our company, Click Industries, started affordable-book-editing.com, where a standard copy edit costs $.009 per word (10% less than any publisher listed in this book). Unlike all the publishers covered here, we don't have tremendous overhead costs, so all of the excess fluff the other guys pass on to writers is turned into savings for you.

The only way to assess the validity of a publisher's up-front fee is on a case-by-case basis (which I do for you in Chapters 6, 7, 8 and 9).

4. Generous Royalties Without Any Fuzzy Math

One of the highly touted benefits of POD is that the author's percentage of royalties is much greater than what a traditional publisher offers.

Unless you're lucky or famous, a traditional publisher offers royalties between 2.5% and 12%. A POD publisher offers royalties from 20% to 80%.

When choosing a POD publisher, the royalty percent is an important factor. Given that most of your sales are going to come as a result of your own marketing efforts, there may be times when a higher publishing fee that comes along with a higher royalty percentage may be worth it.

Publishers calculate the author's royalty percent differently. In many cases, 15% of the gross and 30% of the net may end up to be the same amount. I'd choose a publisher that pays royalties based on the gross sale price of a book instead of the net sale price, which is where fuzzy math plays a role. If your royalty is based on the net sales price, the calculation rarely favors you.

All publishers subtract the cost of the book before calculating the royalty. Most PODs use a printer in Tennessee named Lightning Source to print their books. The publisher pays approximately $.013 per page and $.90 for each cover. For each 230-page book, it costs a publisher $3.89. Knowing this information might be the most important thing in my book, not only in seeing which publishers lie to you about their production costs, but also in determining whether the price at which you can purchase your books for resale is reasonable.

When you ask a publisher about its royalty calculation, the first thing you must ask is where the books are printed. If Lightning Source prints them, tell the publisher you know the actual cost of the book; if they tell you the cost is something higher than that, demand justification. Many PODs build in extra profits on the "cost" of producing each book. Until now, they knew you had no way of figuring out what they were paying for each book. Now you do.

Net vs. Gross Royalty Percentages From Book Sales Through The Publisher's Online Store

You want to find a publisher that pays a royalty based on a fixed percent of the gross sales price less the printing cost. Period. If your book sells for $15 through POD Publisher X's web site and the cost of printing the book is $6, you should make $4.50 on each book sale if you've negotiated a 50% royalty.

Some publishers deduct the credit card processing charge incurred for each transaction (1.5%–2.9% average). I'm okay with this because you still know what you're being paid and why.

The publishers who pay based on a net price (other than taking the gross sales price and backing out the cost of production and credit card processing fees) can be problematic. These guys often define "net price" however it best suits them. A "net sales price" royalty that subtracts the production cost of the book and then bases the royalty percent on that amount is acceptable only if the publishers tell you the cost to produce each book. Still, the problem with this approach is that you'll have to trust their numbers. But now that you know what the publisher pays to produce a book, don't trust anyone.

The only time including additional fees to the raw publishing cost is acceptable is when the publisher takes no royalty or handling fee for the sale of your book. Dog Ear Publishing and BookPros follow this rule: both slightly mark up the cost of the book in lieu of taking any royalties.

The subsection below discusses trade discounts given to third party retailers like Amazon.com as an incentive for them to sell your book. Some of the publishers covered in this book have the gall to give their own online store a trade discount! Don't worry,

I tell you about the ones that do—in my book they're scum. A trade discount is usually 40% to 55% off the retail price. Let's say Publisher XYZ offers its authors 50% royalties based on the gross sales after production cost and the trade discount to all booksellers including its own online store. If the retail price of the book is $15, and the production costs are $5 per book, then the next $5 goes into Publisher XYZ's pocket as the "trade discount" for carrying the book that you've paid them to publish. That leaves $5 to be split equally between you and Publisher XYZ. Publisher XYZ walks away with another $2.50 (for a total profit of $7.50 plus whatever it made off the printing fees) while you make $2.50. See how shady this is?

Finally, stay away from any publisher that arrives at the "net sales price" by deducting vague items such as "administrative costs" and "marketing costs."

Royalties Paid By The Publisher For Sales By Third Party Retailers

When Publisher XYZ lists your book for sale on Amazon.com, BarnesandNoble.com, or any other third party retailer, the money the retailer makes comes from Publisher XYZ's "trade discount," which is usually 50% (although Amazon.com takes 55%). Whether your publisher pays you based on the gross or on the net sales amount, when calculating the royalties for sales made by third party retailers, the trade discount will always be taken off the top first.

In order to compensate for the steep trade discount, PODs usually sell an author's book for a significantly higher price on web sites such as Amazon.com than on its own web site. And no, you will not make more money from sales at Amazon.com. In most cases, you will make less. That is the cost of putting your book for sale with the big online booksellers.

The best deal you'll get here will be if the publisher calculates your royalty percent based on the gross amount it receives from Amazon.com less the production cost of the book (the production cost should only come into play for a print book).

The Royalty Calculation Checklist

Each publisher covered in this book is dealt with extensively when it comes to the factors I believe are most important when determining if the royalty percentage the author receives is as good as the publisher wants you to think it is. Some of the royalty percentages are just as the publisher's represent them to be, but some border on blatant misrepresentation. One goal of this book is to make it harder for unscrupulous publishers to fool writers.

To determine whether the proposed royalty percent is acceptable, evaluate:

- The publisher's method of royalty calculation: is it based on the gross or net sales amount; and if it's based on the net sales amount, the calculation should rely on hard numbers such as production costs and credit card processing fees and not on vague items such as administrative costs
- The actual production cost of the book: production costs on POD books should fall between $.013 and $.015 per page and $.90 to $1.00 per cover
- The size of the publisher's distribution network and traffic to the publisher's online store: more visibility for your book means more sales
- The publisher's marketing efforts to inform readers of your book

5. Low Printing Costs and High Production Value

A publisher can pay the highest royalty percent in the world, but if per book production costs for a paperback drives up its retail price north of $15, the book is probably over-priced. Why expect a casual reader to pay $19.95 for your paperback thriller when the reader can pay $7.95 for a Grisham thriller? Make sure the publisher prices your book in the "retail comfort zone" of the average reader who's willing to take a chance on an unknown author.

Keeping a 250- to 300-page paperback in the $15 range is about as good as it gets in the POD world, where production costs are generally much higher than books printed in runs of several thousand or more. Remember, your publisher doesn't print a copy of your book until it is ordered; this is much more expensive than mass printings, and is the major disadvantage to using a POD publisher.

As I said earlier, in order to stay in the $15 ballpark, the production costs can't exceed $5 or $6. Any publisher that tells you the per book production costs are higher is gouging you and building a tidy profit on the printing end.

Most PODs use Lightning Source to print and ship books. If you haven't already received your money's worth from this book, the payoff is here. Publishers typically pay about $.013 to $.015 per page and $.90 per cover for each book ordered. A 230-page paperback costs the publisher approximately $3.89. Lightning Source receives $3.89 whenever a reader orders your book from Amazon.com. It also receives $3.89 if you order 100 books for a book signing.

Guess how much the publishers typically charge for each book the author buys? Almost all charge more than $8.50 for your 230-page book. What's the publisher doing to earn the extra $4.50? Phoning or e-mailing in an order. Yeah, that's right. Only BookPros and Dog Ear Publishing add an extra 10%-15% to the actual printing cost when their authors order a book. That's a fair mark-up.

If you want to make any money from books that you resell yourself, don't sign a book contract until you negotiate a great purchase price for yourself. These publishers are killing themselves to sign authors. Only the knowledgeable authors know to negotiate a better price for the books they may purchase. If the publisher refuses, move on to another publisher. Make sure you tell them that you know how much it really costs to print the book at Lightning Source. Add 15% to the cost and give them that. If they don't take it, smile and take your business (and your knowledge about printing fees) elsewhere.

With all of this talk about production costs, don't forget about production value. The book must look nice. The cover must be clear, not blurry or cheap looking. The book must withstand multiple reads. The best way to determine the publisher's production value is to order one of its books before signing the contract.

6. Favorable Contract Terms

Before you sign any publishing contract, you need to make sure the contract contains the following provisions:

- A way for you to terminate the contract within 30–60 days
- A clause that states that you own all the rights to your work and any derivatives of your work, such as movie rights
- A clause that requires the publisher, upon termination of the contract, to provide you with all computer and other files that contain the cover art, the layout of your book, and so forth

Contract terms are more detailed that what I've outlined above, and are discussed in Chapter 4.

7. Fairly Priced Additional Services

When considering add-on services, keep in mind that you're entering a gouging zone. Four main areas where rip-offs occur are cover design, editing services, copyright registration services, and printing of promotional material.

Cover Design

A custom cover is essential, so figure its cost into your calculations. Some publishers include a custom cover design in their publishing packages. Avoid any cover template in which you add a picture, photo, or graphic. Your book will look cheap and self-published (or at least what people think a self-published book looks like).

Prices for a custom cover range from $200 to $2,000. It is so subjective, that I can't say that a $2,000 cover is always a rip-off or that a $200 cover is always a great deal. You need to examine sample covers created by the publisher's artists before you decide on the artist. Viewing the covers online may not accurately portray how they look in hand. Request that the publisher send you a book designed by the cover artist whom you intend to hire.

In publishing this book, I asked potential publishers to send copies of their books so that I could see the quality of the product. I assumed that each publisher would send its best example of cover art. In my judgment, some samples were horribly amateurish. Perhaps the cover was not good because a specific author chose to make it that way. In my opinion, the publishers with great covers (and cover artists) are BookPros, Dog Ear Publishing, Infinity Publishing, Xulon, and Booklocker. That is not to say that other publishers don't have excellent cover artists. In fact, I visited Infinity Publishing and BookPros and viewed scores of covers, so I feel confident in the quality of the book covers produced by these two companies.

If you're looking for an affordable alternative to book cover design, check out affordable-book-covers.com, where for approximately $200 to $500 (depending on the artist) you receive top-notch design work without paying a fortune.

Editing Services

There are several levels of editing services:

Copyediting involves correcting errors in spelling, grammar, punctuation, and syntax.

Line Editing is copyediting on steroids—a detailed line-by-line process to correct errors in spelling, grammar, and punctuation. The editor will also make suggestions to improve syntax and word choice.

Content Editing ensures the general accuracy and consistency of content and focuses on more extensive restructuring of sentences.

Before using the editing services of any publisher, make sure you speak with the editor and verify the editor's qualifications. Find out your editor's level of experience. Some publishers use college students and interns as editors.

For a copy edit, don't pay more than $.01 per word. If you do, you'll only be padding the publisher's pockets. A reasonable line edit costs between $.015 and $.02 per word. A fair price for a content edit is between $.034 and $.044 per word.

Editing is not something you can do yourself or skip if you want to put out a professional product. You must have your book edited. What you don't need to do is pay more for this service then you have to. In response to editorial price gouging, my company, Click Industries, started affordable-book-editing.com (mentioned earlier). We have contracts with several highly skilled and experienced editors who provide copyediting services for $.009 per word. For a 150,000-word manuscript, you'll pay $1,350 instead of $1,500 or more.

Remember, don't overpay for editing services.

Copyright Registration

Copyright registration is important, especially if you think you have a book that may really sell well, thus becoming a target for those who may want to misappropriate your work. By registering with the U.S. Copyright Office, you are eligible for statutory damages and attorneys' fees in the event that someone steals or otherwise uses your work without your express permission. For more details on the benefits of copyright registration go to http://clickandcopyright.com/what_copyright_protection_do_i_get.asp.

Many publishers include copyright registration as part of their publishing packages. This service is worth $100 and should include the US Copyright Office filing fee, so when you're calculating your publishing costs, take that into account. Any publisher that charges more than $100 for copyright registration services is gouging you (AuthorHouse charges $150). Publishers that pad the price are likely padding prices for other services.

As you may know, one of the flagship web sites of our company is copyright registration service, Click&Copyright (clickandcopyright.com). We charge $97 (which includes the US Copyright Office filing fee) to draft and file a copyright registration. Here's a tip: type in FINEPRINT when prompted for a promotional code on clickandcopyright.com/copyright_your_book.asp, and you pay only $77 for the service.

8. Ability To Obtain an ISBN, UPC Bar Code, and LCCN As Part of Any Basic Publishing Package

An ISBN number, UPC Bar Code, and LCCN (Library of Congress Control Number) are explained below. The publisher should obtain these three numbers as part of its basic publishing package. If you're required to obtain these items on your own, you might as well self-publish.

Some PODs provide these services à la carte, but be wary of the charges. I've provided a list of services and the maximum price you should pay.

The International Standard Book Number (ISBN)

The International Standard Book Number (ISBN) is a 10-digit number which uniquely identifies books and book-like products.

The ISBN allows libraries and bookstores to find information about the author, the author's book, the book's price, ordering information, and other related information.

You'll need an ISBN to sell your book through any online or offline bookseller. Each edition of a book, whether in paperback, hardcover, ebook, audio or other such form, requires a separate ISBN.

Almost all of the publishers in this book purchase ISBNs in blocks (the smallest is a block of 10). The publisher then assigns an ISBN to an author for each edition of the book the author has licensed it to publish. The ISBN attached to the book lists the publisher as the party to contact for information.

If a publisher wants you to pay for your own ISBN numbers, never pay more than $23 (since you are buying the numbers from them and they are buying them in bulk). If the publisher charges more than $23, you'd be better off obtaining the ISBN on your own and listing yourself as the contact person. This allows you to take your ISBN with you when you terminate your relationship with the publisher.

If the publisher obtains the ISBN for you, and you later terminate your relationship with the publisher and decide to self-publish, you'll need to get new ISBNs for each edition you plan to sell.

If you purchase your own ISBN, you can either purchase a small block of 10 for $225 plus a $24.95 processing fee. If you purchase a block of ISBNs you can assign them to any versions of any books you write (e.g., if you write three books and each has an ebook, paperback, and hardcover edition, you'd use 9 of the 10 ISBNs purchased). However, the only publisher I know that will let you use your own ISBN is Booklocker.com.

You can complete the entire process online at http://www.isbn.org/standards/home/isbn/us/secureapp.asp. A non-priority application takes about 10 days to process.

Keep in mind that if you purchase your own ISBN, most PODs won't allow you to use it for the version of the book they publish. However, you will be able to then publish your own version of your book either during or after the term of your contract with the publisher.

Once the ISBN has been assigned to a book, it should be reported to R.R. Bowker, the database of record for the ISBN agency. Your book can be listed for free in Bowker's Books In Print, so long as you submit the information about your title at www.bowkerlink.com.

If any publisher wants to charge you for submitting your book's information to Books In Print, let them know that you know there is no fee.

UPC Bar Codes

All books use the Bookland/EAN bar code because it allows for the encoding of ISBNs. Almost all book retailers and wholesalers require the Bookland/EAN bar code somewhere on the back cover of a book because this is what the retailer scans at the point of sale to identify the price and information from the bookseller's database. Like any other bar code, the computer then automatically reports the price to the cash register.

If you're interested in learning the meaning of the numbers in a bar code, go to:

www.barcode-graphics.com/info_center/bookinfocontent.htm.

For mass market books, which are sold in drug stores, department stores, and other non-bookstore retailers, a UPC bar code will likely be required since these non-bookstore retailers are not properly equipped to scan the Bookland/EAN symbols (this isn't something you need to worry about if you're published by a POD or epublisher that doesn't sell your book in such venues).

Bar codes can either be on a film master (a negative or positive piece of film), an EPS file (an electronic file that can be provided to printers/graphic designers, so that they can include the bar code within the cover design), or on pre-printed labels utilized when an item or packaging has already been printed or requires unique identification.

The publisher should take care of the bar code without requiring you to pay any fees. If you are using a POD publisher that provides bar code services as an à la carte service, never pay more than $25.

Prices vary by supplier. Accugraphix (www.bar-code.com), one of the larger companies that provide this service, sells a film master bar code for $24 (plus tax and shipping) and an EPS file for $29 (total).

Bar Code Graphics (www.barcode-graphics.com), another large provider of bar code services, charges $15 for either a film master or EPS bar code symbol. It also offers the option of creating your own bar codes (EPS only) online for $10 at www.createbar-codes.com.

Although you don't need to purchase a bar code by a vendor in your home state, a state-by-state list of Bookland/EAN bar code suppliers can be found at www.isbn.org/standards/home/isbn/us/barcode.asp.

Library of Congress Control Number (LCCN)

The Library of Congress Control Number (LCCN) is a unique identification number that the Library of Congress assigns to titles most likely to be acquired by the Library of Congress.

Librarians use the LCCN to access the associated bibliographic record in the Library of Congress's database or to obtain information on various book titles on other databases.

The publisher prints the LCCN on the back of the title page in the following manner: "Library of Congress Control Number: 2001012345."

Only U.S. book publishers are eligible to obtain an LCCN. To receive an LCCN, publishers must list a U.S. place of publication on the title page or copyright page, and maintain an editorial office in the country capable of answering substantive bibliographic questions.

There is no charge for registering, but the publisher must send a copy of the "best edition" of the book for which the LCCN was pre-assigned (you apply for the LCCN prior to publication) immediately upon publication to: Library of Congress, Cataloging in Publication Division, 101 Independence Ave., S.E., Washington, DC, 20540-4320. The "best edition" of a book is the retail paperback or hardcover version of the book.

Books published in electronic form are ineligible for an LCCN.

Should you wish to obtain an LCCN on your own, the first step is to complete the Application to Participate and obtain an account number and password, which takes one to two weeks. The application is online at http://pcn.loc.gov/pcn/pcn007.html. Complete information about the LCCN process can be found at http://pcn.loc.gov/pcn/pcn006.html.

A publisher may try to tell you that there is a fee for an LCCN or that it has to charge you a fee because it needs to obtain one for each edition of your book. Don't believe the publisher. Unlike an ISBN, the LCCN is assigned to the work itself and doesn't change with each new edition or version.

9. Ability To Register the Author's Book with Bowker'sBooks in Print, Make It Available Through a BookDistributor like Baker & Taylor or Ingram, and List It On Amazon.com, BarnesandNoble.com, and Other Large-Scale Sellers

Most PODs have a relationship with one of the major book wholesalers: Baker & Taylor or Ingram. If you want to make your book available in brick-and-mortar bookstores, it must be available through one of these wholesalers. This doesn't necessarily mean that your book will be carried in any bookstore. It means that your Aunt Mabel can walk into her local Barnes & Noble Bookstore and order a copy of your book.

Also, in order to increase your sales opportunities, make sure your publisher lists your book on Amazon.com or BarnesandNoble.com. Everyone knows Amazon.com and should someone hear about your book, chances are that person isn't going to know or remember the URL of the publisher's online store. The first instinct of many consumers when looking for a book online is to go to Amazon.com or BarnesandNoble.com. Making your book available through Amazon.com makes your book appear more legitimate in the eyes of many consumers. Another important reason to list your book on Amazon.com is that if you ever start to really sell books, a traditional publisher considers Amazon.com's sales figure to be more accurate than sales figures from your publisher's web site. The downside of selling only on Amazon.com is that you will make considerably less in royalties per book than you would from sales through your publisher's web site.

Other online retailers such as Borders.com, Powells.com, and BooksaMillion.com, are worthy candidates to make your book available for sale, but first make sure it's available on Amazon.com or BarnesandNoble.com.

As of September 2005, Alexa.com's traffic rankings put Amazon.com as the 13th most visited web site in the world. BarnesandNoble.com was at 503, Booksamillion.com was at 11,669 (still pretty good), and Borders.com was at 369,922.

Regardless of whether a person ever walks into the local Barnes & Noble and asks to buy a copy of your book, you want that option to be there.

Any POD or epublisher claiming to provide a complete publishing service will have your book listed with either Ingram or Baker & Taylor, and will make it available for sale at Amazon.com or BarnesandNoble.com.

As you read the individual publisher profiles, keep in mind these nine qualities that all good PODs should have.

CHAPTER 4

The Fine Print of Publishing Contracts

Lawyers have often been accused of creating a language which only they can understand. This legalese forces the layperson to hire a lawyer who can decipher a document written in this funky little language. It took me three years of law school and many years of practice, which involved drafting hundreds of contracts, to approach these documents with ease.

The contract terms discussed in this chapter are common in most POD contracts. Each publisher uses different verbiage in its contract, so one publisher's termination clause may differ slightly from another, even though the clauses mean essentially the same thing.

The idea here is to help you recognize and understand the various contract terms when you read through the contract of any publisher whose services you're considering.

Specific provisions and problems of each publisher's contract which I feel are significant are discussed in detail in each publisher's profile. I also suggest ways to make the clauses more advantageous by either persuading the publisher to omit or modify certain language, or in some cases finding another publisher.

Surprises are fine, but not in publishing contracts. My number one goal is to help you understand what you sign.

READ THIS CAREFULLY RIGHT NOW, THEN READ IT AGAIN: If a publisher refuses to let you see a copy of a publishing contract before you make a payment, even $1, run away as fast as you can. If a publisher doesn't want you to see what it wants you to sign, take it as the big, fat clue that it is.

Now that we have that out of the way, here are some general provisions found in most POD publishing contracts:

Parties to The Contract

This will always be you (the author) and the publisher. This introductory language identifies names which appear throughout the contract.

The author will often be referred to as the "Author," and not by his or her name.

The publisher will often be referred to as the "Publisher" or "Company," and not by its name.

Your manuscript will usually be referred to as the "Work," and not by its title.

License of Rights

This is one of the most important provisions in any publishing agreement because it states the precise rights the author licenses to the publisher during the term of the contract.

In most POD contracts, the author grants either an exclusive or a non-exclusive license during the contract term. An exclusive license prevents anyone who is not the license holder, including the author, from publishing the author's book in the format for which the right is being licensed. A non-exclusive license allows others, such as the author or other publishers, to sell, distribute, and publish the book during the contract term.

If you're having your book published as an ebook, you will grant the publisher either an exclusive or non-exclusive right to print, publish, and sell your book in an electronic format, which typically includes such formats as a downloadable ebook, a CD-Rom, or a format that can be read on a Palm Pilot, Microsoft ebook Reader, or other similar device.

If you're publishing your book as a paperback or hardcover, you will be granting those specific rights. Granting paperback rights does not automatically include hardcover. Contract language which describes "all print rights" includes print and hardcover rights.

Some publisher contracts are for "worldwide" rights. During the term of the agreement, the publisher can sell your book anywhere in the world in the format(s) you've agreed upon.

Some publishers only ask for rights to sell the book in the United States, Canada, and the United Kingdom. For example, if a publisher only has print rights in the United Kingdom, the author would still have the right to sell, distribute, and publish the book in print anywhere else in the world.

Print and electronic rights are the only rights that should ever be at issue in a POD publishing agreement. Stay away from a contract that grants the publisher "all rights whatsoever." Giving these rights to your publisher includes your claim to subsidiary rights, which include movie, television, radio, or stage play rights.

One publisher, Enoval, used a contract with these rights. I warned the company owners that their unfavorable contract would be their demise. The company is now out of business.

Stay away from any publisher that demands an option or right of first refusal on any other books you may write. It's one thing if you sign a three-book deal with a major publisher and receive payment up-front, but it's an entirely different matter in the POD world.

Many PODs specifically state that they are not claiming an interest in any other rights other than those directly related to the publication of your book. It's not required or necessary language to have in a contract, but it does make your rights indisputable.

Term and Termination

The term and termination provisions are just as important as the license of rights. The term defines how long the contract will last. The termination provision describes what either party must do to cancel the contract and when they must do so.

The term and termination sections are often written together as one provision. It is important to read the license of rights and the term and termination provisions together to determine whether a contract is author-friendly. In each publisher profile, I always discuss these three provisions together when analyzing a particular contract.

Look For Contracts That Have Terms That Do Not Lock The Author Into A Contract For A Long Period of Time

The most author-friendly POD publisher contracts will have these terms:

- Exclusive, but only for one year
- Exclusive for X years, but the author can terminate at any time by giving X days written notice or
- Non-exclusive for X years and author can cancel at any time

There are, of course, a few exceptions to the general rules. The goal is to always have the least number of restrictions on your rights, freeing you to search for a better publishing deal with a traditional publisher or third party.

If a publishing contract you're considering doesn't have a term like one of the three described above, then you should think long and hard before signing. If you attempt to terminate a contract that doesn't have a term like one of the three above, you're not going to be a happy camper.

Avoid Contracts That Permit a Publisher To Retain Non-Exclusive Rights After Termination

Avoid any contract that grants the publisher a non-exclusive right to publish and sell your book after contract termination.

I'm not talking about contracts that permit the publisher to sell its remaining inventory of your book after termination. Besides, a POD publisher should have fewer than ten books in its remaining inventory.

Here are two unacceptable situations:

A. The publisher receives an exclusive term for one year, which the author can cancel at any time during that year. But if the author cancels the contract before the term is up, the publisher retains a non-exclusive right to sell the book through the original one-year term.

B. The publisher receives a two- year, non-exclusive right, which allows the publisher to publish, distribute, and sell your book during that time period regardless of what you do.

The problem with both situations is that the author isn't in full control of his or her rights. The ability to sell your book while someone else continues to sell it is not the same as having full control of your rights. Suppose a big-time publisher, such as Random House, wanted to purchase rights to your book. Before dealing with Random House, you had signed a contract under scenario A or B. Although you have the right to sell Random House your licensing rights, the POD publisher's non-exclusive rights remain effective. Once Random House learns about the POD publisher's rights, it quickly loses interest. At best, Random House would first have to purchase the POD publisher's non-exclusive rights before it would purchase any licensing rights from you.

From the POD publisher's perspective, the non-exclusive right is worthless unless a traditional publisher decides to publish your book. It's unlikely that the POD publisher will actively market or sell your book. When Random House enters the picture, that POD publisher's rights to your book become valuable. The POD publisher will sell its non-exclusive rights to the author or Random House, or it will publish as many books that it can sell. What you want to avoid is a situation where your POD publisher is suddenly a factor in your negotiations with a traditional publisher.

You must address these non-exclusive contract provisions, which are present in many POD contracts (including Hyperbooks), in one of these ways:

- Remove the language that gives the publisher non-exclusive rights after termination
- Modify the language to permit the publisher to sell any remaining inventory it has as of the termination date, but prohibit the publisher from printing and selling additional copies after the termination date
- Modify the language to give the author the right to purchase the publisher's non-exclusive rights upon termination for an amount equal to the publisher's net profit from sales it would have made during the non-exclusive period. The net profit should be based on the net profit during the previous X months (equal to the term of the non-exclusive period after termination would be). For example, if the publisher had a non-exclusive right to sell the book for a year after termination, then the buy-out price should be based on the net profit during the year that proceeded the termination date. Define the net profit as the retail price of the book less production costs, author royalties, and trade discounts
- If I terminated the agreement to sign with a bigger publisher, I'd nonchalantly try to buy the POD publisher's non-exclusive right before signing the new contract with the bigger publisher

Avoid Contracts Whose Terms Extends
For the Length of the Copyright

If you learn only one lesson from this book, remember this: **NEVER, EVER, UNDER ANY CIRCUMSTANCES, ENTER INTO A CONTRACT WHOSE TERM EQUALS THE LENGTH OF THE COPYRIGHT.**

A copyright term lasts for the life of the author plus another 70 years. This allows the author's heirs to receive your copyright's benefit after you're gone. Once you sign a contract whose term extends for the life of your book's copyright, you've lost control over your work forever.

Watch out for publishers that try to back-door such a provision into a contract. For example, Protea Publishing may try to sneak such terms into the contract. Its standard contract leaves the term undefined. Your only out is if it fails to pay royalties for one year.

Pay Special Attention To Terms That Renew Automatically

Some publishing contracts have an initial term of X years which automatically renews on a year-to-year basis until terminated. Oftentimes, termination requires the author to give notice at least X days before the expiration of the initial or renewal term. In theory, there's nothing wrong with this requirement.

In practice, it may prove tricky. Let's say you signed a one-year agreement on January 1, 2006, which renews automatically on a yearly basis unless terminated 90 days before the expiration of the initial or renewal term.

If you want to terminate the agreement after the first year you must give notice at least 90 days before December 31, 2006, or by September 29, 2006. If you gave notice on November 15, 2006, the publisher could require you to honor the automatic renewal term through the end of 2007.

Automatic renewal clauses exist for your convenience as much as for the publisher's. Without the clause, the publisher must stop selling your book and remove it from its web site at the end of the initial or renewal term. To resume sales and earn more royalties, you would have to notify them of your desire to extend the contract.

Most PODs include renewal clauses. The best way to avoid a problem is to schedule a reminder on Outlook or other calendar system before the deadline passes.

Author Warranties and Publisher Indemnification

Warranties

Author warranties are promises the author makes about the submitted work. These warranties are usually the most intimidating provisions of any POD publisher contract because of their lawyerly sounding language.

Author warranties can be summed up like this: don't break the law or violate anyone else's rights in your book and you'll be okay.

I've listed eight author warranties commonly found in POD contracts and supplied explanations of their meanings. Not all publishing contracts contain all eight warranties, nor will the language match exactly, but I've provided enough information for you to get the gist.

Author warranties:

1. **"Author is the sole author and proprietor of the work."**

   If another writer has any interest in the book, other than a writer that you paid to provide certain services such as ghost writing, you cannot make this representation unless you have a written agreement with the other writer in which he or she has agreed that you are the sole author and proprietor. Examples of individuals who may have an interest in your book are co-authors and illustrators.

2. **"Author owns all rights in the work free of any liens and encumbrances and has full authority to enter this agreement."**

This clause expands on #1, and confirms that no one else has, will, or can make a claim to any of the rights. For example, if someone sued you for copyright infringement and the case was ongoing at the time you signed the publishing contract, the lawsuit would be an encumbrance because you would not have the ability to sell your work in its present condition until the lawsuit was favorably resolved.

3. **"The Work is original and has not been previously published."**

This one is self-explanatory. The work is your own and not created by another person, and the work hasn't been published anywhere else. If you have published the work previously, make sure you inform the publisher so that this clause can be amended.

4. **"For work not in the public domain legally effective written licenses have been secured."**

This section means that for any work not in the public domain (something you can use because the copyright protection has expired) you are warranting that you've obtained legal permission to use it.

5. **"No part of the work, including the title, contains any matter which is defamatory, unlawful, or which in any way infringes, invades, or violates any right, including privacy, copyright, trademark, or trade secret of any person."**

It's easier to break this one down by giving examples:

- If your book claims that your neighbor, John Smith, is a child molester, then that would be defamation, unless the claim is true. Truth is always a defense to defamation.

- If your book instructs people how to blow up government buildings, most publishers consider this instruction to be unlawful, regardless of your First Amendment Rights.

- If you put your girlfriend's private diary in your book without her permission you are violating her right to privacy and infringing on her copyright in her diary. If you take a portion of this book and use it in your book without obtaining my permission, you've infringed on my copyright.

- If your book has Harry Potter as a character, you've infringed on J.K. Rowling's copyright and trademarks. However, stating that a character drank Coke or appeared on CNN isn't considered infringement.

- If you print Coke's secret recipe in your book, you've infringed on Coke's trade secret (its recipe).

6. **"The publication doesn't breach any oral or written agreement the author has made with anyone else."**

You are confirming that you don't have any other agreement with any publisher or third party in which you licensed the same rights.

7. **"The representations and warranties are in full force and effect on the date of publication."**

You are promising that all representations and warranties you made will be true on the publication date as they are on the day you signed the contract.

8. "The warranties survive the term of the Agreement."

This means that if you defamed someone in your book who then sues the publisher several years after the publishing agreement expired, you will still be liable for the representations and warranties you made.

Indemnification

When you indemnify a publisher you are saying that if any warranties you made turn out to be false, you will cover all of the publisher's legal expenses if it gets sued.

Here are three typical indemnity clauses you may see in publisher contracts:

> "The author indemnifies and holds the publisher harmless from any losses, expenses, or damages arising out of or for the purpose of resolving or avoiding any suit, demand, etc., as a result of the author's breach of the representations and warranties."

If you used someone else's copyrighted material in your book, all legal expenses incurred by the publisher, any damage awarded by a court, and any settlement amount the publisher makes to avoid a lawsuit, will ultimately be paid by you.

It's simple. Make sure your representations and warranties are true, or prepare for a legal mess should a third party sue.

> "The Publisher can extend the benefit of the Author's representations and warranties and indemnities to any party affected by the Author's breach."

If the publisher sells your book through Amazon.com, and the person defamed in your book sues Amazon.com, the representations, warranties, and indemnifications you made to your publisher will also cover Amazon.com. You'll be responsible for Amazon.com's costs, attorney's fees, losses, damages, and more.

> "Author has to pay legal fees, costs, etc., to defend any suit brought against the publisher as a result of the Author's breach of any representation or warranty."

This language is usually included in the first indemnification clause mentioned earlier. The publisher may choose to set it apart so that it's crystal clear that the author is responsible for the publisher's legal fees and expenses if the author breaches representations and warranties.

Permission and Releases

Some contracts include this section:

> "Provided there is a legal review of the final, complete manuscript of the work, the Author, at the Author's own expense, agrees to obtain from any person or entity from whom, in the publisher's opinion, permissions, releases, or licenses shall be required in order to exercise the rights granted hereunder . . . ."

If your characters work at XYZ Cafe, and XYZ Cafe happens to be a real restaurant in the city in which the story takes place, the publisher may require you to secure written permission to use the cafe's name from the establishment's owner.

Use of Author's Name and Likeness

Language for this type of clause may read like this:

> "The Author grants the publisher and its licensees the right to use the Author's name and likeness in the sale, promotion, and advertising of the work . . . ."

Granting a publisher the right to publish your book doesn't automatically give it the right to use your picture or name on its web site or a third party's web site, or in retail stores where your book is for sale. This clause gives the publisher permission to use your name and picture in the marketing and promotion of the book.

Publisher Bankruptcy

Many POD publishing contracts include this clause:

> "If the publisher commences bankruptcy proceedings, all rights to the work shall immediately revert to the author."

This clause protects the author. All assets of a publisher who files for bankruptcy become the property of the bankruptcy trustee. Without this clause, the license you gave to the publisher under the publishing agreement also becomes the bankruptcy trustee's property. This creates problems for the author because the author must then deal with the court-appointed person handling the publisher's affairs.

In some bankruptcy situations, the publisher "reorganizes" and continues to run the company. Bankruptcy clauses in the publishing contracts, however, don't differentiate between the various types of bankruptcy.

In theory, the second the publisher files for bankruptcy protection, all of the author's rights immediately revert to the author. In reality, the clause may not be enforceable. The automatic stay provision of the bankruptcy section of the U.S. Code (11 U.S.C. §362(3)) controls. The provision states that upon filing for bankruptcy, a stay applies to any act to obtain possession of property of the estate or of property from the estate or to exercise control over property of the estate. Of course, a creditor can always apply for relief from the stay, but for an unsecured creditor like an author, good luck. When a publisher files for bankruptcy, most bankruptcy trustees return the rights to authors in exchange for the authors' agreement to drop any claims for all unpaid royalties or other monies due.

Notices

Notice provisions explain how the author and publisher must provide notice of events or situations requiring notice, such as termination of the contract.

Some termination clauses permit notice by fax, e-mail, or regular mail. Others require notice by certified mail only.

If a contract requires delivery of notice in a specific manner, you must follow that manner for the notice to be effective. For example, if a contract requires notice to be sent using certified mail and you fax the notice, your notice is not legally effective.

Governing Law; Venue; Attorneys' Fees

These clauses are sometimes combined in one clause and entitled the way I have done so above. If your contract lacks a separate clause, look for relevant language in the "General Provisions" or "Miscellaneous" contract clauses.

In the example below, I use Minnesota and Hennepin County (Minneapolis). The counties and states will be different depending on the location of the publisher. The clause may read like this:

> "This Agreement will be construed and controlled by the laws of the State of Minnesota, and each party consents to the exclusive jurisdiction and venue by the state or federal courts sitting in the State of Minnesota, County of Hennepin. If either the publisher or author employs an attorney to enforce any rights arising out of or relating to this Agreement, the prevailing party will be entitled to recover reasonable attorneys' fees and costs."

Let's break it up to review each point:

1. Governing Law

> "This Agreement will be construed and controlled by the laws of the State of Minnesota. . . ."

Should a legal dispute arise, the court will use Minnesota's case law and statutes to interpret the provisions of the contract.

Usually the state laws where the publisher or its lawyers are located will be used to interpret contract terms. Why? Because the publisher's lawyers are familiar with the laws of the state in which they already practice. The publisher won't be billed extra fees while its lawyers learn the nuances of another state's laws.

There are times when a publisher may choose to have the contract governed by the laws of another state because a particular state may have a statute or law more favorable to the publisher.

For your purposes, the publishing contract clauses discussed in *The Fine Print of Self-Publishing* cover basic contract law principles, and the differences among state laws are minimal.

2. Venue

> ". . . and each party consents to the exclusive jurisdiction and venue by the state or federal courts

> sitting in the State of Minnesota, County of Hennepin . . . ."

This provision specifies that if one party sues the other party for a contractual breach, the lawsuit will be brought in the state or federal court located in the state identified in the agreement—in this case, a state court in Minnesota or federal court in Hennepin County, Minnesota.

Without the author's consent to a specific venue in the state of the publisher's choosing, the publisher could have a difficult time suing the author in that state. By agreeing to sue and be sued in the state of the publisher's choosing, the author cannot sue the publisher in the author's own state (unless it's the same state) because once the publisher's lawyers show the court the contract, the case will be thrown out.

3. Attorneys' Fees

> "If either the publisher or the author employs attorneys to enforce any rights arising out of or relating to this Agreement, the prevailing party will be entitled to recover reasonable attorneys' fees and costs."

I call this provision the "keep-it-honest" clause because it makes a party think twice before filing a lawsuit. Without a solid case, you will likely pay 100% of the publisher's attorneys' fees. The reverse is also true. These "prevailing party" clauses are fair.

Some publishers try to sneak in language that says: (1) the author pays the publisher's attorneys' fees regardless of the case's outcome, or (2) the publisher recovers its attorneys' fees if it prevails in a lawsuit but the author cannot. Many publishers get away with this tactic because people don't bother to read these clauses before signing the agreement. The party who drafted the contract banks on the other party overlooking it.

While I've yet to encounter an unfavorable attorneys' fees clause, I've seen these exact clauses in other commercial contracts.

Request elimination of the unfavorable attorneys' fees clause or a modification to a "prevailing parties" clause, and most publishers will agree rather than risk losing you as an author. If the publisher refuses, then it's time to find another publisher. A publisher's reluctance to change this clause indicates the company would rather strong-arm me than work with me.

An inequitable attorneys' fees clauses makes it financially difficult, if not impossible, for you to pursue legitimate claims against a publisher. To me, that is unacceptable.

Entire Agreement

"This Agreement constitutes the entire agreement between the Publisher and the Author with respect to the subject matter hereof and supercedes all prior written or oral agreements made by the parties. This agreement may not be modified or amended except in writing and signed by both parties."

Virtually every commercial contract I've seen includes this standard clause, and I've never drafted a contract without including it.

Look for this clause as a separate section entitled, "Entire Agreement," or as part of the "General Provisions" clause.

What is written in the contract are the only terms that count. Nothing said and nothing written prior to the execution of the contract is valid or enforceable. If you received an e-mail from the publisher telling you that the royalty is 50% of the gross, and the contract you later sign states a royalty of 30% of the net, the prior written communication by the publisher is meaningless.

If you could show that that 50% was an inducement to get you to sign the contract and that it was fraudulent, you might be able to get out of the contract. Maybe. But, how far are you willing to go and how much money are you willing to spend to compensate for not reading and understanding the contract?

Read the bold language in this paragraph continually until it is branded in your brain: Carefully read the contract and make sure it is complete. It must include every promise and representation by the publisher, whether oral or written, based on your review of the publisher's web site and any other relevant information.

If you believe the written contract is different or incomplete from what you understood it to be, DO NOT SIGN the contract until you are absolutely satisfied with the written terms!!!!!!!

General Provisions/Miscellaneous

Often, the governing law, venue, attorneys' fees, and entire agreement clauses may all be part of the "General Provisions" or "Miscellaneous" provisions. Here are three additional clauses typically found in these contract provisions:

> "Author may not assign this Agreement or any rights or obligations hereunder, by operation of law or any other manner, without Publisher's prior written consent, such consent which will not be unreasonably withheld."

This language prevents you from transferring your rights under the contract without the publisher's permission. However, the publisher can't unreasonably refuse permission if you request to assign your rights. For example, if you're assigning your rights to the new corporation you formed or to your wife, the publisher should agree to your request. If you assign your rights to another publisher, you'll probably encounter resistance.

> "If any term or provision of this Agreement is illegal or unenforceable, this Agreement shall remain in full force and effect and such term or

> provision shall be deemed deleted or curtailed only to such extent as is necessary to make it legal or enforceable."

If a court finds a portion of the contract illegal and unenforceable, the rest of the contract remains valid. The problematic term will need to be deleted or rewritten to make it comply with the law.

> "No modification, amendment, or waiver shall be valid or binding unless made in writing and signed by all parties hereto."

I've already covered this, but it bears repeating. If you and the publisher orally agree to change your royalty percentage, the agreement will carry no weight and remain meaningless until it is put in writing and made an addendum (addition) to the original publishing contract. Both you and the publisher must sign the new agreement.

CHAPTER 5

Analyzing The Fine Print of Each
Publisher's Contract and Service

In an earlier version of this book, all publishers were given an author-friendly rating between 0 and 10. That system differentiated between a 9.4 and 9.7. The differences become minute and subjective, and some publishers started using their rankings to advertise themselves as the highest-rated company in my book. As a result, excellent publishers ranked at 9.5 were overlooked by writers because writers focused on publishers ranked at 9.8.

I now have an author-friendly ranking that groups publishers by category. The four categories are:

- Outstanding
- Pretty Good
- Just Okay
- Publishers to Avoid

The factors used to determine a publisher's ranking have evolved. I contacted every publisher listed in this book and requested responses to these questions. The answers to these questions critically impact a new author's success:

1. What is the retail price of a 230-page book (without any special graphics, etc.) with a full color cover?

2. What percent of royalties is the author paid for sales through your web site and sales through third parties like Amazon.com?

3. Is the book price printed on the book?

4. What price does the author pay for this book? How is the price determined? (e.g. $.90 for the cover plus $.015 per page).

5. What is the shipping charge on books the author purchases for resale (author copies)?

6. What is the bookstore discount? The Amazon.com discount?

7. Do you offer authors the opportunity to participate in Amazon Advantage?

8. Are authors paid a royalty on books they purchase themselves?

9. Do you allow bookstore returns? If yes, what charge, if any, do authors incur?

10. Are your book covers laminated?

11. Where are your books printed: in-house, overseas, or through a third party printer?

12. Do you offer live customer service support for your authors? If so, is it done in this country or overseas?

13. Do you offer any marketing support to your authors besides selling bookmarks and other printed materials to them?

14. What price, if any, do you charge to maintain an author's book on your web site?

15. How fast do books ship to both the author and the consumer?

The retail price of the book. The average reader who peruses Amazon.com and finds a novel by an unfamiliar author will probably not spend $22 for it. People who argue otherwise live in a fantasy world. Who is going to spend $22 on your book (other than your friends or family) when Patricia Cornwall's thriller costs only $7.99? Some PODs build in hidden profits in the retail pricing structure of their books. It's my goal to uncover these ploys.

The price the author pays for the author's books. Another biggie. Aggressive marketing of your book is essential to the book's and your overall success. Companies that allow you to purchase books in the $5 to $8 range score high. Yes, if you went to an offset printer, you could get books for a few dollars each. But if you don't want a garage stacked full of books, a POD publisher is the smart alternative. If you can buy your book for $5 to $8, then you can sell it for $12 to $15 and make money. Few things irk me more than publishers who charge a ton of money up front, and then gouge you when you purchase copies. I've asked every publisher for the price of a standard 230-page book with a full color cover. This factor plays in big.

Allow bookstore returns. I believe an author can successfully sell books through personal appearances, the author's web site, and Amazon.com and other online retailers. An author's chances of success, however, increase greatly when bookstores have the ability to make your book available other than by special order. Most bookstores won't consider buying a new author's work, and virtually all bookstores won't if the publisher doesn't accept bookstore returns. You must find a publisher who accepts returns from bookstores. Many publishers charge approximately $400 to agree to bookstore returns. Some publishers include bookstore returns as part of their packages.

Customer support for authors. You're a customer of the publisher. You paid them money for a service—to publish your work—and as a customer, you should be able to call them with questions. Your book is a personal and important achievement. You're entitled to talk to the people you've entrusted it to and not someone in New Delhi who knows little about your book.

Author-friendly contract terms. Author-friendly publishing agreements contain most or all of these provisions:

- Authors grant only print and electronic rights on a non-exclusive basis, which is terminable at any time, or for an exclusive term, which is terminable at any time or extends for less than one year
- The publisher doesn't retain a right of first refusal or other such option on any future books, and the publisher doesn't require payment from the author in the event the author signs with a bigger publisher or sells television or movie rights
- Authors can terminate the contract easily and with no further obligation
- Upon termination by the author, the publisher only maintains a limited non-exclusive right to sell any of the author's remaining books the publisher has actually printed;
- Upon termination, the author receives the cover art, layout, design, and more—all products which the author has made payment on;
- Calculation of royalty amounts based on a percentage of the retail price of the author's book or, if based on a percentage of the net price, the calculation is clear and not subject to padding
- Competitive pricing of the author's book in the marketplace
- No requirement that the author pay the publisher's attorneys' fees in the event of a dispute, except for defamation or the author's misrepresentation as to ownership of rights. Clauses that require the non-prevailing party in a lawsuit to pay the prevailing party's legal fees are equitable

Based on these factors and a few intangibles, such as how fast the publisher's responded to my requests and the quality of the books they produce, I grouped the publishers into one of four categories.

For easy reference, I've listed publishers alphabetically within each category. The order is not a ranking within that particular section.

CHAPTER 6

Outstanding Self-Publishing Companies

The publishers in this category are simply the best in the business. Understand that not every publisher in this section is right for every writer, but there is a publisher here for just about everyone. Both the most expensive and one of the least expensive self-publishing companies made this list. One self-publishing company operated by a large corporation made this list, as did one of the new comers to the industry.

All these companies share a proven commitment to author-friendly policies. Five of the outstanding publishers, after speaking with me, modified their contracts to make them more author-friendly. They all get it. It's about understanding writers. Writers treat their books like they treat their children. Their books are dreams fulfilled, and often represent a lifetime of work. These publishers don't nickel-and-dime you to death. Instead, they work with you to achieve the results you want.

While every company is in business to make money, these publishers also provide great services at fair prices.

BookPros, which is by far the self-publishing company with the highest up-front fees, made this list because it produces exceptionally crafted books and offers writers publicity equal to that of the best traditional publishers. One self-publishing giant, iUniverse, made this list because over the past several years it has worked hard to provide writers with what they want and need.

Booklocker offers the lowest initial publishing fee, yet it manages to publish aesthetically pleasing books. Xulon, the only Christian publisher to make this list, put together in the last year a wonderful program which balances religious beliefs and marketing savvy.

Perhaps the most important characteristic shared by these publishers is their commitment to providing better and more relevant services. Each publisher answered all of my questions, examined practices that were less author-friendly, and some changed these practices, once again proving their commitment to superior products and services.

BOOKLOCKER
http://publishing.booklocker.com/

FORMAT OF BOOKS: ebooks and POD

GENRES ACCEPTED: Accepts all genres of nonfiction and fiction. Accepts 30% of all submissions and only publishes quality books, as the bulk of their money comes from selling books.

PUBLISHING FEES: Free for ebooks. $199 for POD, plus $18 per year hosting fee.

You can either supply your own cover or have them create a customized cover for $99 (via a template) or $199 (original design). Provides generic cover art for the ebook.

Includes an ISBN, unless author supplies own (makes moving your book to a new publisher simpler since the ISBN provides the order information, and if you use one of Booklocker's numbers, they will be listed as the contact. It's no problem, but you'll need to get your own ISBN if you terminate your agreement with Booklocker).

ROYALTIES PAID TO AUTHOR: 70% of the list price on ebooks that retail for $8.95 or higher; 50% on ebooks that retail for less than $8.95.

The royalty for print books sold through Booklocker's online store is 35% of the list price. If your book is sold through Amazon. com or other third parties, you receive about 15% of the list price.

NOTABLE PROVISIONS OF THE PUBLISHING AGREEMENT: The contract can be found at www.booklocker. com/contract/contract.txt, It is one of the longest around, yet quite harmless.

Section I makes it clear that the contract is non-exclusive.

Section II (5th paragraph from the end) requires the author to terminate the contract with Booklocker prior to entering into another contract. Author can terminate instantly via e-mail.

Section V sets forth publishing fee information.

Section VI provides pricing guide information for hardcover and paperback books. The last paragraph in Section VI confirms that the author is free to sell the book on his own. However, as long as you are under contract with Booklocker you agree to not sell the book for less than the price Booklocker sells it.

In Section XVI, in the third to last paragraph, any lawsuit against Booklocker must be brought in Bangor, Maine, and the forum will be binding arbitration. This is not an unreasonable clause, and is quite standard in all commercial contracts in which one party drafts the document. Yes, they want to give you every disadvantage possible if you contemplate suing. It's likely that litigating in Bangor, Maine, will prove more costly than the disputed amount.

TIME FROM SUBMISSION TO PUBLICATION: POD authors receive their print galley within four to six weeks after submission of the final manuscript. Ebooks are ready sooner. They will let you know within five days after you submit a book whether they want to publish it.

ALEXA TRAFFIC RANK: 94,839

AUTHOR-FRIENDLY RATING: As close to perfection as you're going to find in the world of ebook and POD publishing.

The ebook royalties are the highest I've ever seen, and the print royalties are better than average.

It's simple to terminate the agreement at any time. Your rights are always with you.

The $199 POD fee is reasonable. Booklocker understands what new authors experience, and have put together a package that is the best in the business. You can't go wrong here.

Plus, they're selective and won't publish any manuscript just because it's accompanied by a $199 check. Also, the web site is well trafficked.

If you can find a POD or epublisher with as much integrity and dedication to selling authors' books, but with lower POD publishing fees, please let me know.

BOOKPROS
www.bookpros.com

FORMAT OF BOOKS: paperback and hardcover

GENRES ACCEPTED: Acceptance is selective. While any genre could be accepted, BookPros only takes on books it believes it can promote effectively. So a book has to be a real gem before this company will consider it, as it will not promote books to its media contacts that aren't of a similar quality as those it is representing from major publishing houses. BookPros actually started as Phenix & Phenix Literary Publicists in 1994 and became a prominent publicity firm before venturing into self-publishing, printing and design and ultimately renaming itself in 2005. Publicity remains

BookPros' foundation and focus, and each book they review is evaluated based on its perceived media potential.

PUBLISHING FEES: range from $6,000 to $40,000. This company is not cheap, and they make sure that you go into the process with your eyes open. They don't promise huge sales or national fame and are very up front about whether they feel like they are a good fit for a certain book. They do have the ability to produce finished products that rival any book put out by Random House, Dell, or any other big-time publisher and have the industry relationships to give your book a great chance at success.

BookPros has four publishing packages:

Great Reading Books

BookPros' basic package costs around $6,000. While expensive, it is actually a good value for the money. If you plan to do something more than selling your book to family and friends, you would need to do the things offered in this comprehensive package anyway, so you might as well do them under one roof and under the direction of experts who promote books for the same publishing houses you hope someday to be signed with.

Includes the following services:

- US Copyright Office registration

- ISBN and EAN barcode

- Registration with R.R. Bowker's Books In Print

- Registration with book wholesalers so that your book can be ordered by any bookstore.

- Listing your book on BN.com and on Amazon.com

- Drafting of an AP Press Release, a broadcast press release, and an author bio

- Editing

    Unlike 100% of the other PODs in the world, Book-Pros requires that your book be professionally edited before they'll print one copy. Again, they won't attach their name to something that doesn't look and read like it came out of the biggest New York publishing houses. Unlike most PODs that do offer editing, the editing here is done by seasoned book editors, not college students or interns. In fact, BookPros has a person whose job it is to find the best editor for your book. An editor who specializes in romance novels will not be editing your travel book. A basic edit of grammar, syntax, etc. is $5.00 per page with a minimum of 220 pages or $1,100. A full edit including plot, characterization, etc. is $7.00 per page. So, a 400-page book you have in Word, will cost $2,800. If there is a bargain here, this is it, and it's a biggie! If you go hire a book editor on your own, you'll be paying between $.01 and $.015 per word just for a grammatical edit (so on that 400 page book, it'll be around $1,000). The extra $1,800 or so for a full edit including plot, characters, etc. is simply a great deal.

- Layout

    If you open a book printed by most PODs, the layout may look fine. But what a book reviewer or other experts will notice is a layout that screams POD.

    Book Pros' layout services are $1,045 for 220 pages and 4.75 per page (for books that don't have images) after that. I'm no expert in the layout of books, so I asked BookPros to justify $1,045 for the layout of your book. Here's the response:

It is actually a lot more detailed and tedious than just "pushing a button." Each page has to be formatted, so the headers and footers correspond correctly as well as eliminating any widows and orphans. If there are subsections throughout, this too will add more time. Granted, not all books have subsections, but that doesn't free the designer from going page by page to ensure everything is in order.

In addition to the above, the layout designer must review each line of the document to make sure no spaces have been added before a paragraph begins (which typically passes by the editor and author), take out any tabs that may have been placed when writing the document etc.

At any given time or at any given step, something can be altered that wasn't meant to be. So it does take time to ensure such things do not occur.

All I can tell you is that I paged through many of their books, and the entire thing was a model of excellence. With BookPros you are buying a Cadillac instead of a Honda Civic. When a seasoned pro opens up your book, what do you want them to think? That's what this comes down to. You can get this service cheaper, but again, you get what you pay for. If you're investing in your career, then it doesn't make sense to skimp on anything. That being said, I don't claim to be an expert on book layout, so from a technical standpoint I can't tell you whether the layout is so much different from a $200 layout to justify the cost.

- Cover Design

   In terms of strictly selling books, the cover is the number one most important aspect. It is what captures the attention of the eye in the bookstore and what makes a book stick out.

A basic cover design costs $1,050. This is higher than any other POD publisher, but again BookPros is in a different league. A custom cover costs about $2,850 and includes a stock photo image.

Can you get a great cover for less? Absolutely. Can you pay less than what BookPros charges and get a cover that makes your book look like Random House published it? Nope. BookPros contracts with some of the top book designers in the US. These people aren't cheap.

I examined dozens of books published by Book-Pros and was blown away by the covers.

If you're serious about your career as an author, suck it up and invest in a great cover. That's the bottom line.

- Press Materials Sent to 500 Media Contacts

  So many PODs offer a service like this, but it's a joke and rip-off. Here's how most of these work—a fax or mass e-mail is sent to the same general media list that the POD publisher sends every press release to. So, the romance novel press release and the Vietnam War autobiography press release go to the same media contact. Which means that 95% of these are tossed in the trash or deleted without ever being read.

  Naturally, I was skeptical when I saw that Book-Pros offered this service. On behalf of any author who might think of spending thousands to publish his/her book, I pressed BookPros hard on this one. I sat down with one of BookPros' managing partners, who showed me the sophisticated database of 450,000 plus media contacts divided into hundreds of categories and sub categories. Impressive. A publicist at BookPros searches this extensive database looking for media contacts who actually want to hear about books like yours. Then depending on how big the list, they narrow it even further to ensure that a press release about your book ends up in the hands of a person who is already interested in the subject matter.

An extensive database like this is worth a lot and along with the editing, justifies much of the $6,000 in fees. Think about how long it would take you to find 500 journalists and book reviewers interested in works like yours. Plus, the press release is coming from a real publicist, not you.

TurnKey Press

This package is for the author who wants an authentic book publicity campaign. There will be additional fees involved depending on how long of a PR campaign you choose.

You get everything you get in the Great Reading Series package, plus:

- Book submitted to Amazon Search Inside and Google Print Program

- Custom Press Kits

    Five hundred full-color press kits (custom designed folders) and 2,000 sheets of letterhead (breaks down to four various pieces of 500 each), which are sent to media contacts. These press kits are just like the ones the big-time publishers give out.

    This will cost you about $2,000—$2,500. You can find hundreds of places on the internet where you can learn how to create your own press kits, but if you want BookPros to handle the media for you, they do it the only way they know how—first class. Plus, they only slightly mark up the materials. So is it worth a slight mark-up to have a professional take care of everything and design the media kit the way the media likes them? Just the time it takes you to run around and do everything piecemeal is worth $300. If $300 is an issue, then this company is not for you.

- Media Prep Sessions

    You are assigned a media campaign manager who will strategize the best approach for your book's publicity.

    You will also fly to Austin and conduct mock media interviews in a Media Training session.

    Media prep is actually the first month of every publicity campaign with BookPros. This is the portion of the campaign where the team is writing press materials, researching competitive titles, targeting specific media outlets, conducting strategy development and doing Media Training. Professional firms spend time plotting a course for the campaign before beginning to contact media.

    When you are at this level and wanting to make writing a career, this is one of the many things you have to do.

- Media Campaigns

    BookPros will also recommend a length for the campaign, and you have the option to do that specific campaign or anything shorter, depending on budget. Most campaigns start out between two to six months. Each month is about $3,500, and the fees per month decrease the longer the campaign is. Here the publicist working on your book will contact local and regional print, radio, TV, online and other media outlets and then follow up. This includes getting book reviews, TV and radio interviews, online media opportunities, and much more.

    The media campaigns are expensive, but they are the same type that BookPros conducts for the major publishers. McGraw Hill, Random House, Broadman

& Holman, Time Warner, Thomas Nelson, Entrepreneur Press, HCI, Howard Publishing and many other publishers have hired BookPros (some when they were Phenix & Phenix) to handle the media for newly released books.

If you want a publicist that knows what to do and how to get results, use the company the pros use. If you want to hire a local publicist who may not specialize in books, then do that, but you'll end up spending a lot of money, with probably less than satisfactory results.

You won't have the option to even engage Book-Pros for a publicity campaign unless a team of publicists and others at BookPros determines that your book has a chance of making it. BookPros would be out of business in minutes if authors were paying thousands of dollars for minimal results. If you need to be convinced that these people know what they're doing, visit the office and view the number of accolades that cover the walls.

In addition, visit their website, where you will find a list of media they have booked with through the years, a number of case studies that shed light on specifics from previous campaigns and some articles that have featured their publicity team.

Bridgeway Books

You get everything in the TurnKey Press package in addition to:

- National Direct Wholesale Distribution

- Opportunity to print books on an offset press
  For authors looking to step outside of many of the problems that normal POD distribution brings to the table, this imprint may be a good way to do it. Bridgeway Books is the first self-publishing imprint, that I am

aware of, that has obtained direct distribution through Ingram. What this means is that the books published through this imprint will have an actual stock at Ingram, preventing bookstore managers from having to special order books as they do for POD. This isn't to say that your book will be on shelves around the country, but it does give you access to those shelves so that BookPros' publicity and your own marketing efforts have the ability to pay off. Bridgeway Books are also featured in Ingram's catalog, which goes out to bookstores across the country.

This imprint is a nice step option for authors who are looking to avoid the infamous POD stigma. You can print anywhere from 500 to 2,500 books, which leaves a good amount of inventory available to sell at speaking engagements and other events. Since you have the opportunity to print books offset, all of a sudden your can go hardcover and do other creative things with the design of the book without pricing yourself out of the market. The flip side is that you must print an inventory, and the budget required to do so may not make this imprint a good option for first-time authors. This is key, because since the budget must be high for an author to publish on this level, it is not likely that BookPros will accept you for this imprint unless you have the ability to sell a certain amount of books direct. They don't want to attach their name to a book that isn't going to sell. On top of that, part of the advantage of being able to print a stock of books is having inventory available to sell in the back of the room.

Synergy Books

If your book is not phenomenal (as judged by professionals, not your friends and family), you won't even be considered for this imprint. A book MUST have the potential to be promoted nationally before BookPros will attach a Synergy Books logo to the book.

Synergy Books is a hybrid between pure self-publishing and traditional publishing, in that the author fronts all the publishing costs, retains control and rights and makes all the money, but the books are promoted and distributed in a similar fashion that they would if published by a traditional publisher.

This will cost you $35,000 to $40,000, but it is the only way to truly do it right, if you are going to self-publish. The distribution, design, printing quality and PR available through the imprint are on par with anything that you will get at a major traditional house.

This is a similar publishing schedule that a traditional book would be on and the exact same type of service. High- quality distribution takes time, so if you need the book out in four to six months, this isn't a good option for you.

In addition to all of the things you get in the other three packages you get:

- 2,500 copies of your book

- National media solicitation for interviews, etc.

- Distribution through Biblio/NBN (a large book distributor) that will pitch your book to Baker & Taylor and Ingram (the big wholesalers), Barnes & Noble and Borders, independent bookstores and regional wholesalers for six months. So, salespeople armed with copies of your book will be hitting the pavement trying to sell your book for major distribution.

I've only scratched the surface here, so don't think that you just get 2,500 books for all that money. If you ever get the chance to visit BookPros and feel the excitement and electricity in the office, you'll feel good about the money you spent.

ROYALTIES PAID TO AUTHOR: You aren't actually paid a royalty, since BookPros isn't actually selling your book, but rather distributing it through sites like Amazon, wholesalers, master distributors, etc. Actual figures are discussed below.

NOTABLE TERMS OF THE CONTRACT: The contract isn't available online, so just ask for one if your book is accepted. The first several pages spell out the services being provided and the price. If you are unclear about any of the services, you should request a clarification, to ensure that you are getting what you believe you paid for.

No matter what package you purchase, you're paying a lot of money, so make sure the contract is clear to you with regard to the services being rendered.

Section 4 states what you will be paid upon a sale for either the Great Reading Books imprint or the TurnKey Press imprint. Since you set the price (with the assistance of BookPros' publishing staff), the actual amount will vary from author to author and will depend on the printing cost of each book. For books sold through distributors, you will receive the wholesale cost of the book, less the production cost, less a 15% service equal to the production cost.

On books you purchase for resale by you, you will pay the cost of production plus 15% of that cost. If you buy the books in huge print runs of 1,000 or more, you'll obviously pay less. If you purchase on a print on demand basis, you will pay more in actual dollars, since the production cost is more.

Let's take a 200-page book. You will pay $.90 (for the cover) + $3 ($.015 x 200 pages) + $.45 (15% service fee) or $4.35 per book. If you are selling your book for $12 to $15 you will still be making more than you could ever make under any traditional publishing contract.

Since each imprint has a different distribution/wholesale distribution arrangement, the amount that you make for sales differs. Through Bridgeway Books, an author can expect to receive 45% of the retail price of the book for retail or online sales through online retailers. Through Synergy Books, an author will received slightly less—40% minus $1—since the book is actively distributed by sales reps for Biblio/NBN. With both of these imprints, a real focus should be on direct sales because an author keeps all profits from direct sales (whether in the back of the room, on your website or on a bulk sale that you secure to a business or other organization).

Section 8 deals with who owns the intellectual property. Not only do you own the book (story, etc.) but you also own the layout, the design, the cover art, etc. So, you can pull your book any time from this publisher and have it published by someone else whenever you want. Many PODs keep the design, formatted version of the book, etc., so if you go to another publisher, you will be paying all those expenses again. You'll pay BookPros a lot, but it's all yours. If you choose to publish elsewhere later, you won't have to pay anything other than printing fees.

Section 12 is the all-important termination clause. Either party can cancel with 60 days' written notice. If BookPros cancels, it will return all monies you paid that have not been spent in the production of the book. If you cancel before the entire contract is completed, you will be refunded all monies you paid for service not yet rendered (If you terminate before the publicity campaign starts, that money will be refunded to you).

BookPros was one publisher that changed a portion of its contract I found objectionable (Section 12, subsection 4). Under it, if you canceled within three days of signing the contract, Book-Pros could keep $500. For many authors, finding the money to invest in this type of project is not something to be taken lightly. In those few days after signing, if an author realizes he/she can't afford to proceed, there shouldn't be a penalty. BookPros agreed with me and removed this clause.

ALEXA TRAFFIC RANK: inapplicable here since BookPros doesn't sell through its own online store.

AUTHOR FRIENDLY RATING: You can't rate this publisher against all the others in this book. If you are a recreational writer or not ready to make your book a significant part of your career plan, BookPros is not for you. Unless you are 100% invested in your career as writer, BookPros is not for you.

Of course, when I saw some of these prices, I immediately thought rip-off. Believe me, I was skeptical. I imagined a boiler room with dozens of closers getting praise-starved writers to write out huge publishing checks. Unlike most of you, I was able to visit BookPros and see for myself what was really happening.

They have an 8,000-square-foot office, bustling with energetic, and dedicated employees. The woman whose job it is to guide authors through the production process told me she's reading three books at any one time—just for pleasure. The point is, you want to be with a company made up of people passionate about publishing and reading. BookPros is that company.

BookPros' $6,000 package is the closest to any POD publishing package covered in this book. Yes, it's $4,000 more than the most expensive publishing service discussed here. So why would I rank this company so high? Simple. BookPros does what no other publisher covered here does—they make you do a first-class job before they'll publish you. No other self-publishing company requires your book to be edited. If you are serious about your book, you have to have it professionally edited. That adds between $1,500 to $2,500 to your book regardless of whom you choose as a publisher. The 500 press releases are sent to media contacts who are actually interested in a book like yours. Plenty of PODs have the mass e-mail press release where the press releases are just sent to some generic list. For my money, a real targeted press release distribution to 500 willing media contacts, coming from a respected publicist, is worth at least $1,500.

For those of you who really want to focus on your writing career, if you can afford a book publicist, why not go with a proven winner? These people have been promoting books for HCI, Broadman & Holman, McGraw Hill and others. They know what they're doing. You can engage their services for as little as a month.

I've said it before in this review, if you're ready for the big leagues and have big-league talent, but no way to break in (can't find an agent), then this company is for you. You'll spend money up front, but the rewards will all be yours.

I asked the president of BookPros, Mike Odom, this question: "You have a big operation here and need to pay the salaries of a lot people. If I came to you with the worst book ever written, but handed you $50,000 to publish and promote it, you'd do it wouldn't you?" Mike's response: "We'd lose all our credibility in the industry if we did."

Friends, that says it all.

COLD TREE PRESS

www.coldtreepress.com

FORMAT OF BOOKS: paperback

GENRES ACCEPTED: all

PUBLISHING FEES: The Semi-Custom Package $900 (http://www.coldtreepress.com/publish/choice1.html) includes:

- Customized cover
- ISBN and Bookland EAN bar code
- 5 finished author copies of the book
- Ebook formatting and online ebook sales
- Registration at Books In Print
- Registration and sales through Amazon.com, Barnesand-Noble.com, and booksamillion.com
- Ability for your book to be ordered through bookstores

The Custom Package $1,200 (http://www.coldtreepress.com/publish/choice2.html) includes:

- All features of the Semi-Custom Package
- Individually designed and formatted cover and interior text
- ISBN number and Bookland EAN bar code
- Library of Congress Registration
- U.S. Copyright registration
- Author Sell Sheet
- 10 finished author copies of the book

The Combination Package $1400 http://www.coldtreepress.com/publish/choice3.html includes:

- All features of the Custom Package
- Your book as a hardcover.
- Personal interaction throughout the production process
- 10 finished hardcover copies and 5 paperback copies of your book
- Books In Print registration
- Free Marketing Design Assistance
- Direct access to the publisher's CEO for help in further design and marketing issues.

ROYALTIES PAID TO AUTHOR: 30% of the retail list price for sales made directly by Cold Tree Press to the reader and 15% of retail list price for sales made through third party retailers.

NOTABLE PROVISIONS OF PUBLISHING AGREEMENT: The publishing agreement can be found at http://www.coldtreepress.com/contract/index.html

Section 4 and Section 8 grant non-exclusive rights to the publisher for one year, but either party can terminate at any time with 30 days written notice. After an author's cancellation, the publisher has 90 days from the end of the month in which the cancellation occurred to sell all remaining copies of the work.

Section 6 representations, warranties, and indemnifications are standard and reasonable.

Section 7 clarifies that the publisher only provides printing and book sale services.

Section 12 requires any lawsuit arising from a dispute between the parties to be brought in Davidson County, Tennessee.

ALEXA TRAFFIC RANK: 550,418

AUTHOR-FRIENDLY RATING: The contract contains author-friendly terms: short, non-exclusive, terminable by the author at any time, and decent royalty percentages.

In the earlier version of this book, I rated this publisher low because the cost of its publishing packages. I've since reconsidered. The publisher produces beautiful covers. Company founder and CEO, Peter Hornsberger, explained why his $900 package was worth it by pointing me to a section on the company's web site:

> "Each book is individually designed and formatted based on the content of the book itself. We use no templates—each book is custom from start to finish. The interior text and formatting, including the cover concept, is specifically designed for the content and genre of your book. We provide three initial custom cover designs to choose from, as well as initial formatting of the interior that you approve prior to the complete formatting of the book.
>
> This cost is all-inclusive. There are no extra charges for corrections, cover designs or formatting. We don't force you to use what we may design initially; we work with you until you are satisfied. Period. If you already have a concept that you want executed, we can do that too. You will also

work directly with the person who will be designing and overseeing your book from manuscript through publication. No associates.

As it is being formatted, we take the time to adjust the spacing on each line, if necessary, to reduce hyphenation, eliminate widows and bad line breaks. We believe in our work and that of our authors. That's why we put forth that extra effort. We think the end result is worth it.

Many authors have put years into writing their book, we think the end result should reflect that same dedication."

Peter Honsberger is also an award-winning graphic designer. His work has received recognition from various organizations and publications, including the New York Art Directors Club, Communication Arts Magazine, Print Magazine, the National Advertising Federation, and the International Poster exhibition. Honsberger shows his dedication to authors and their works by putting out well written and aesthetically pleasing books.

In return for more up-front costs, you receive hands-on cover design work, which includes three separate original designs, and careful formatting of your book.

This publisher tries to be as accommodating as possible. A clause in the original contract granted rights to the book's cover art and layout to the publisher in the event of an author termination. After a conversation with Honsberger, that portion of the contract was deleted.

Cold Tree Press is an up-and-coming self-publishing company. With its author-friendly philosophy, its model will be one that other publishers should follow.

DOG EAR PUBLISHING
www.dogearpublishing.net

FORMAT OF BOOKS: Paperback or Hardcover

GENRES ACCEPTED: All

PUBLISHING FEES: There are three publishing packages:

Basic Package $699.00 (http://dogearpublishing.net/pricingbasic.aspx), which includes:

- Custom interior and cover design with up to 5 images
- Up to 10 free paperback books or 5 hardcover (dependent upon format and page count)
- Book and author web page in the Dog Ear Publishing web site which links to a sales page at Amazon.com or author's web site
- Registration with all major online booksellers and national distributors
- Registration with Books In Print database providing worldwide availability
- Assignment of International Standard Book Number (ISBN)
- Library of Congress registration (LCCN)

Professional Service $1,499.00 (http://dogearpublishing.net/pricingpro.aspx), which includes everything in the Basic package (or upgraded feature below) plus:

- Up to 30 interior graphics and 10 tables (supplied by the author)
- Up to 20 free paperback books or 10 hardcover books (dependent upon format and page count)
- Marketing and promotional support including:

> -Personalized domain name
> -Custom web site, which Dog Ear manages for one year.
> -E-mail marketing campaign to your database of up to 500 addresses
> -Press Release to 100 targeted media outlets
> -5 posters, 100 postcards, and 100 bookmarks

The marketing services are invaluable. Not only do you get a personalized domain name, but for an additional $150, Dog Ear will also build a shopping cart if you want to sell books yourself and not pay a huge discount fee to Amazon.com.

The e-mail marketing campaign portion isn't worth much because you still must compile the list.

However, Dog Ear uses some of the same tools that top public relations people use to customize a press release campaign for you. This is no cookie cutter project.

Masterpiece Package $3,499 (http://dogearpublishing.net/pricingprem.aspx), which includes everything in the Professional Service package (or equivalent upgrade below) plus:

- Total Design Customization that includes up to 100 interior graphics and 20 tables (supplied by the author)
- Up to 75 free paperback books or 30 free hardcover books (dependent upon format and page count)
- Professional editing and proofreading
- Aggressive Marketing Campaign that includes:
  1. Press release to 500 targeted media outlets
  2. 250 promotional cards with a picture of your book and ordering information
  3. 100 post cards for mailing with a picture of your book and ordering information
  4. 10 posters showing your book, your picture, and ordering information

    5. Regional Author Signing and Sales Campaign, including New Book Announcement

    6. Sheets distributed to 100 regional outlets, combined with follow up phone calls soliciting Author Appearances and book orders.

Yes, this is a lot of money, but editing is something you need. You cannot self edit your book. It doesn't work. Dog Ear assured me that all editors are real book editors who edit for a living. Out of the $3,499, that's worth at least $1,300.

You also receive 75 books. At $5.88 per book (for a 230-page standard book), that's worth $441.

The marketing campaign is worth at least $1,000. Add in a customized cover and you're close to $3,500.

ROYALTIES PAID TO AUTHOR: 100% of the retail price of the book less publishing fees and bookstore discount. If you sell the book on your web site, you pay Dog Ear $5.88 and if you sell it for $15.00, you make $9.22.

Dog Ear charges a bit more for author copies compared to other publishers ($1.28 per cover and $.02 per page versus $.90 per cover and $.015 per page), but they take no cut of the retail price, so on a 230-page book, Dog Ear makes no more than $5.88.

Take POD Publisher X who takes a 40% royalty from the sale of a your 230-page book. Assume that it charges an author $.90 for the cover and $.015 per page ($4.35). Also assume the book retails for $15.00. After deducting the cost of the book ($4.35) there is $11.65 to split. The author ends up with 60% of the remainder, or $6.99, as opposed to $9.22 under the Dog Ear model (assuming you handle the book fulfillment yourself).

If you want Dog Ear to handle all book fulfillment, credit card processing, etc., a $2.00 per sale fee is added, but you still come out ahead under that model too.

NOTABLE PROVISIONS OF THE PUBLISHING AGREEMENT: The publishing agreement can be found at http://

www.dogearpublishing.net/resourcesauthoragree.aspx.

The contract is simple and straightforward. The author warranty and indemnification section is standard and reasonable.

Courts interpret contracts in the light most favorable to the non-drafting party (the author), which benefits you if you ever need to sue a publisher for breach of contract. Because this book is author-focused, I'm not pointing out the specific misstep Dog Ear made while drafting the venue and jurisdiction clause (since then they'd change it), but any lawyer with half a brain should be able to figure it out. Trust me, it benefits you.

ALEXA TRAFFIC RANK: 464,000

AUTHOR-FRIENDLY RATING: There is a lot to rave about. The model is a great one. The publisher makes more up-front on each book, but you receive 100% of the net sales price. If you do the math, you'll see that this pricing strategy is advantageous.

The marketing and promotional aspects of the packages are another plus. Forget the posters and cards. Focus on the press release campaign. Dog Ear hand-picks media outlets that would most likely find your book interesting, and sends them professionally produced releases. Dog Ear uses services such as Bacon's and Gebbie Press to compile these lists. These are the same services that most public relations professionals perform.

The Masterpiece Package offers the best value. You get your own web site and domain, which is essential if you plan on selling books yourself.

The only downside is that it takes seven business days for book orders to ship.

The company's three owners are all book industry veterans. One is a former printing broker, another a former buyer for Walden-Books, and the third a former acquisitions editor for Macmillan. Together, the owners have a true understanding of the book business.

Dog Ear is the new guy on the POD publishing block. Don't be surprised if it's around for a long time.

INFINITY PUBLISHING

www.infinitypublishing.com

FORMAT OF BOOKS: POD

GENRES ACCEPTED: All

ROYALTIES PAID TO AUTHOR: 20% on retail sales through publisher's online bookstore, www.buybooksontheweb.com, and 10% on wholesale sales.

For each dollar you add to the suggested retail price your royalty increases by $.75 (www.infinitypublishing.com/royalties.htm)

PUBLISHING FEES: $499, which includes:

- ISBN number
- Bookstore-quality cover
- Title submission to Books In Print database
- Book information submission to third-party booksellers such as Amazon.com
- Title submission to the Ingram database

NOTABLE PROVISIONS OF THE PUBLISHING AGREEMENT: The contract is at www.infinitypublishing.com/popup_agreement.htm.

Paragraph 3, under "The Author," requires the author to register the copyright with the U.S. Copyright Office and provide a copy of the stamped form to the publisher.

Paragraph 7, under "The Author," clearly states that the publisher has no ownership in the work, and that "the author is free to pursue any and all publishing ventures . . . ." You can publish and sell your book anywhere else during the term of the agreement.

Paragraph 9, under "The Author," allows the author to terminate the agreement at any time.

OTHER SERVICES: The publisher offers four marketing packages at a cost of $125 to $470 (http://www.infinitypublishing.com/bookmarketing.htm). All packages include copies of two excellent books, *The Complete Guide to Book Publicity*, by Jodee Blanco and *1001 Ways to Market Your Book*, by John Kremer. All packages include free copies of your book (from 2 to 25). All packages except the $125 package provide posters of your book cover (5 to 25).

You can find Blanco's book for $19.95 and Kremer's for $27.95. The owner of this publisher also owns a commercial-printing operation, so the pricing on bookmarks and posters is probably competitively priced. Whether you need these products is up to you. I'm not an expert in the pricing of bookmarks and posters, so I can't tell you if this is a great deal. I've seen the publisher's work and I can vouch for its professionalism and craftsmanship.

ALEXA TRAFFIC RANK: 363,382

AUTHOR-FRIENDLY RATING: Any serious writer should consider Infinity Publishing. Infinity Publishing is a fantastic operation. The contract is 100% author-friendly and requires no other discussion.

Unlike many other PODs, Infinity runs an in-house publishing operation, not an overseas production. An author can call and speak to an "Author Advocate" who helps in a variety of ways. The Author Advocate provides marketing ideas and tips. The Author Advocate can even walk across the hall to the print shop and report back on the status of your book.

Yes, the $499 set up fee may be higher than some other publishers, but you receive a lot in return. Nothing is contracted out at Infinity. The owner, cover designer, and the person running the print shop take great pride in every book and author. If you want a cover designer whom you can call and discuss your preferences, and if you want quality book bindings similar to ones you'd find at Barnes & Noble, then you pay a bit more. Is it worth an extra $150? Absolutely.

Another advantage is that because this publisher holds publishing equipment valued at over $500,000, it cuts out the middleman and prints books for less cost. The books it prints, including your book, are competitively priced for the market, making it easier for first-time authors to more easily sell their books.

At first glance, the royalties seem low for POD books, but there's no fuzzy math involved. You receive 20% of the sales price if your sell books through the publisher's quality online bookstore. No "net" of "net" type of stuff.

Infinity publishes many authors who successfully sell their books. This success reflects two facts: (1) Top-notch writers who are also sales-oriented seek out Infinity, and (2) Infinity's pricing, cover art, and quality help authors stay competitive.

I toured Infinity's physical operations and went away impressed by its commitment to quality and its hands-on approach with authors. You won't be just a number here.

iUniverse
www.iuniverse.com

FORMAT OF BOOKS: paperback, hardcover, and ebooks

GENRES ACCEPTED: all

PUBLISHING FEES: Has four publishing programs:

The Fast Track Publishing Program: $299 (http://www.iuniverse.com/book-publishing/publishing-fast-track.htm?pro_name=FastTrack) includes:

- Templated cover design
- Sales through iUniverse only

- One copy of your book
- Paperback formatting only

The Select Publishing Program $459 (http://www.iuniverse.com/book-publishing/publishing-select.htm?pro_name=Select2), which includes:

- Custom, four-color book cover
- Ebook set up
- ISBN
- Inclusion in Bowker's Books In Print, Amazon.com, BarnesandNoble.com, and others
- 5 free copies of your book
- Author web page on iUniverse and sales through iUniverse online bookstore.

The Premier Publishing Program $669 (http://www.iuniverse.com/book-publishing/publishing-premier.htm?pro_name=Premier2), and includes all services or products in the Select Publishing Program (or equivalent upgrade below) plus:

- 10 free books
- Editorial Review (http://iuniverse.com/editorial-services/editorial-review.htm), which is not editing but a check of the book's general structure to determine if there are many grammatical errors
- Bookseller Discount Program (http://www.iuniverse.com/book-publishing/book-seller-discount.htm) allows authors to offer traditional booksellers up to a 50% discount, which makes your book more attractive to retail stores.

The Premier Plus Publishing Program $799 (http://www.iuniverse.com/book-publishing/publishing-premier-plus.htm?pro_name=PremierPlus), which includes all services and products in the Premier Publishing Program (or equivalent upgrade below) plus:

- A back cover copy polish in which an iUniverse copywriter will write the back cover.

ROYALTIES PAID TO AUTHOR: 20% of the sales price for print books and 50% of the sales price for ebooks, provided they sales are made through iUniverse. If not sold through iUniverse, royalties equal the payment the publisher receives from a third party retailer, such as Amazon.com, less shipping and handling, sales and use taxes, and returns. If the author opts for the Bookseller Discount, which gives booksellers a 50% discount, then the author's royalty is 10%.

NOTABLE PROVISIONS OF THE PUBLISHING AGREEMENT: The contract for each program can be found at http://www.iuniverse.com/book-publishing/contracts.htm

With the exception of Schedule A, the contracts and the paragraph numbers discussed below are the same regardless of the program.

Paragraph 2, "License to Publish," gives iUniverse non-exclusive print rights in English for three years from the book's release date (Paragraph 5, "Term"). However, the author can cancel anytime during the term by giving 30 days notice (Paragraph 6, "Author Cancellation").

Paragraph 11 allows the publisher 60 to 180 days to release your book.

Paragraph 12 gives the publisher total control over price, appearance of your book, and more. The price for a 230-page paperback is $15.95 for fiction and $18.95 for nonfiction. What will the general public pay for a book by an unknown writer? What price is too high? Why is the price of a nonfiction book $3 more than a fiction book?

Paragraphs 19 and 20 cover author warranties and indemnifications, which are reasonable and standard.

Paragraph 21 explains the manner in which the author or publisher must give notice to terminate the agreement. These requirements must be precisely followed for the termination to be effective and valid.

Paragraph 23, an old copyright infringement section, is troublesome. It prohibits the author from commencing a copyright infringement suit without the publisher's permission. The paragraph also gives the publisher the exclusive right to commence a lawsuit on your behalf. If you fail to participate monetarily in the case and iUniverse later receives a monetary award from the defendant, the author has no right to a share in the proceeds.

Once I pointed out this unfair arrangement to iUniverse, it quickly redrafted this section with the following language:

> "If during the term of this Agreement the copyright in the WORK is infringed, AUTHOR hereby authorizes PUBLISHER, at PUBLISHER'S sole expense, to commence an action for copyright infringement in AUTHOR'S name. Any recoveries from such litigation shall be applied first to reimburse PUBLISHER for its expenses incurred in such litigation and thereafter any remaining balance shall be divided equally between PUBLISHER and AUTHOR. PUBLISHER shall have no liability to AUTHOR if PUBLISHER elects, in its sole discretion, not to commence such an action. If PUBLISHER does not bring such an action, AUTHOR may do so at AUTHOR'S sole expense. Any recoveries from such litigation shall be applied first to reimburse AUTHOR for AUTHOR'S expenses incurred in such litigation and thereafter any remaining balance shall be divided equally between AUTHOR and PUBLISHER."

Paragraph 24 is stuffed with legalese, but don't be intimidated. If a legal dispute arises, such as an issue over contract interpretation, the statues and case laws of New York will be used to interpret the provisions. It also prohibits the author from assigning rights in the contract to anyone else without the publisher's consent. For example, if you decide to incorporate a business, you must first obtain the publisher's permission before assigning the contract rights to your new corporation.

Paragraph 24 addresses circumstances in which specific portions of the contract are judicially determined to be illegal or unenforceable. In such cases, the contract itself won't be invalidated or terminated. Rather, the problematic portion will either be deleted or modified to conform with the law.

The second to last sentence in Paragraph 24 says that any promises or representations made to the author prior to signing the agreement is unenforceable if it's not mentioned in the agreement. If the written contract doesn't resemble the oral agreements you made, don't sign it. Once you've signed the agreement, the only way to alter it is in writing, or it doesn't count. An oral agreement that you and iUniverse made before or during the term of the contract is invalid unless it's memorialized in writing. This is not a negative. All agreements should be in writing.

ALEXA TRAFFIC RANK: 40,110

ADDITIONAL SERVICES: As you can imagine, a giant company like iUniverse offers myriad add-on services. Here are a few worth noting:

- Editorial services (www.iuniverse.com/editorial-services). All levels of editing are available: basic grammar and spelling costs $.015 per word; line editing, which includes suggestions about syntax and word choice and some light structural changes, costs $.018 per word; and content editing, which includes focus on the plot and flow, costs $.022 per word. These fees are in line with the industry average.
- Kirkus Discoveries Book Review Service (www.iuniverse. com/book-marketing/kirkus-discoveries.htm), if requested through iUniverse, costs $360. If purchased on your own, it costs $350, but you would still need to send two copies of your book to the Review. The Kirkus Discoveries Book

Review is a review by this respected publication. Your payment doesn't guarantee a stellar review. If you receive a bad review, you can elect to not have it posted on Kirkus's web site or displayed elsewhere. Requesting a Kirkus Discoveries Book Review lends your book legitimacy from a well-known and respected reviewer.

AUTHOR-FRIENDLY RATING: iUniverse is the 900-pound gorilla of POD publishing. Most writers have seen its glossy advertisement in writing magazines, trade journals, or online ads. If you choose iUniverse, don't expect the hand-holding you'd receive from a smaller publisher.

iUniverse's prices are reasonable. The $699 Premier Publishing Program is the best value.

I have two issues with iUniverse:

1. The author pays too much for copies of the book. iUniverse offers a 20% discount to authors. If an author's book costs $15.95, a 20% discount lowers the book price to $12.76. But add on shipping and handling charges, and he'll need to sell one book at over $15 to make any profit. Because iUniverse prints large volumes, it makes a lot of money on books sold to authors.
2. The 20% royalty is low. The royalty should be at least 35%. A 10% royalty from retail bookstore sales is reasonable, but why does iUniverse make 80% royalty when you've already paid it a substantial sum to publish your book?

What I like about iUniverse:

- It's a company which finally realized the service is about the writer. The proof? I brought to its attention a portion of the contract that was unfavorable. Within 10 days, iUniverse agreed to modify it, resulting in an extremely fair contract. Ability to deal with author-related issues quickly and professionally is as important as royalties and publishing fees. Its publishing contract is now one of the most author-friendly out there.

- iUniverse is a stable company which will likely be around for a while. Its corporate America look, feel, and operation lend credibility.

- Its pricing for services such as editing and Kirkus Book Reviews are fair and reasonable.

- If you start to sell a substantial number of books at iUniverse, you have the potential to be "discovered." This is a service with a successful track record, which no one else offers. This feature is my favorite because as long as you've written a commercial winner, iUniverse can provide the next steps to bring you closer to being discovered.

Through the years, iUniverse has received complaints about its level of service, responses to complaints, and more. It has worked hard to address these problems and deserves recognition for its efforts. Its publishing agreement has also become one of the most author-friendly around.

If you consider this publisher, contact some of iUniverse's mid-level authors and inquire about their experiences with this POD giant.

When weighing your publishing options, iUniverse is a company you need to consider. Although the royalties are low and the price an author pays for books is high, your book will be on a heavily trafficked web site. And, if you have success in book sales, iUniverse has the ability to get you to the next level.

LULU
www.lulu.com

FORMAT OF BOOKS: ebooks and POD (paperback)

GENRES ACCEPTED: All

PUBLISHING FEE: This is a complete à la carte based system. There are no set packages. If you handle the layout and cover design on your own, you can publish through Basic Distribution Service $34.95 (http://www.lulu.com/help/node/view/153), which includes:

- ISBN
- Scannable Bookland-EAN bar code automatically printed on the back cover (not applicable to one-piece covers)
- Listing in Books In Print
- Ability to take your books into the local bookstore for them to sell
- One-year placement in the Amazon Marketplace

If you want to receive similar services offered by other publishers, Lulu provides links on its web site to third party vendors. If you used one of these third party vendors, you would pay about $429 for:

Deluxe Publishing Package $280 (www.lulu.com/content/135690), which includes:

- Cover design (author provides the images)
- Book formatting
- Submission to Amazon.com, Barnes & Noble, Borders, and Booksamillion.

Global Distribution $149 (www.lulu.com/help/node/view/213), which includes:

- ISBN
- Scannable Bookland-EAN bar code automatically printed on the back cover
- Listing in Books In Print
- Ability to take your books into the local bookstore for them to sell
- Book entry into Ingram's database, Titles@Ingram, and Neilsons Bookdata (UK) bibliographic databases. Your book title also made available through Bertrams and Gardners, wholesalers in the UK market.

Lulu offers free images for your use in creating your book cover. For a customized cover, which costs approximately $230, you can use one of the third party vendors listed on Lulu.com (www.lulu.com/category/9010).

ROYALTIES PAID TO AUTHOR: Determined by the author. Go to www.lulu.com/help/node/view/204, and you can see how the royalty is determined and calculated.

For example, suppose you sold your 250-page, 6x9 book for $14. Subtract these costs: $4.53 (fixed fee for cover, binding, and setup) and $5.00 (printing costs at $.02 x 250 pages). What remains is $4.47. Lulu takes 20% of this amount, which is $.90, and you keep the rest (www.lulu.com/help/node/view/204).

Selling your book through online retailers, which take discounts, results in smaller royalties. You may need to price the book differently. If you use the Global Distribution system, the base price of your book is $6.56 ($5.00 at $.02 per page and $1.56 set up fee). Since Amazon takes a 55% discount, you'd need to sell the book for $15.95 to make almost $2.00 per book.

Authors purchase copies of their books for $4.53 per book plus $.02 per page. Shipping is free if the order is between $25 and $100. If you order fewer than 26 books, you pay $9.12 per book.

For orders between 25 and 100 books, you pay $9.05 per book; between 100 and 250 books, you pay $7.40 per book; between 250 and 500 books, you pay $6.69 per book; and over 500 books, you pay $6.30 per book.

NOTABLE PROVISIONS OF THE PUBLISHING AGREEMENT: The publisher's member agreement is available at http://www.lulu.com/about/member_agreement.php. This agreement is used by its writers and web site users. Only portions relevant to writers are discussed.

Section 3 states that Lulu makes no claim to the copyright in your work but has permission to post and sell the author's work. It also discusses royalties: you will be paid the amount you specify per the royalty calculation. This section lists all author representations and warranties, which are reasonable.

Section 8 is significant because it explains how an author removes its work for sale from the publisher's web site. It's a simple process that can be done at any time.

Section 11 allows Lulu to shut down its web site at any time. There is little the author can do about it. But, this is not a big deal. It simply means that if Lulu goes out of business, you don't have any recourse because your books aren't sold through the site.

Section 12 confirms that services to the author are done on an "as-is" basis. If there's a glitch in the system, such as a technical error which prevents your book from being ordered from its web site for ten days, there's nothing the author can do about it.

Section 13 disallows an author's claim for damages resulting from circumstances described in Sections 11 and 12 beyond the amount the author paid Lulu in connection with the transaction giving rise to the claim. For example, if Lulu issues an ISBN that's already issued to another author, you could only sue them for $34.95, the amount you originally paid for the ISBN number.

Section 14 confirms that Lulu owns everything on its web site that isn't submitted by a member.

Section 15, Paragraph 1, requires changes to the contract to be in writing and signed by both parties. Paragraph 2 says that either party who could have made a claim under the contract but didn't does not give up the right to do so later. Paragraph 3 means that if a section of the contract is deemed invalid, the rest of the contract remains valid.

Paragraph 4 points to the laws of North Carolina as the governing authority.

Any dispute will be handled by a single arbitrator and arbitrated in Raleigh, North Carolina. The arbitrator's ruling is final and enforceable in court.

Section 16 states that the agreement continues until either party terminates, but that certain provisions such as warranties survive termination.

Section 17 says that the publisher can change the terms of the agreement at any time and if you don't like the changes you can stop using the web site and remove your work.

ALEXA TRAFFIC RANK: 6,858

AUTHOR-FRIENDLY RATING: If you're looking for any easy, no-frills way to sell your book without high up-front fees, this publisher is for you. For $429, you can buy a complete publishing package.

Lulu offers services similar to other self-publishing companies, but in à la carte fashion. This arrangement offers maximum flexibility.

The agreement is as author-friendly as they come. The ability to set your price is a great feature, and the royalties can be as high or low as you want based on your projections.

The charge to the author for copies of the book is high, especially on orders of fewer than twenty-six. But, if you order more than three, you get free shipping, which lowers your net cost lower than you'd pay at other PODs.

Lulu is a solid company that will probably be around long after many other self-publishers have folded. When considering self-publishing companies, Lulu must be on your list.

OUTSKIRTS PRESS

www.outskirtspress.com

FORMAT OF BOOKS: ebooks, paperbacks, and hardbacks
GENRES ACCEPTED: All

PUBLISHING FEES: There are five publishing packages ranging from $199 to $999. Complete details can be found at www.outskirtspress.com (click the "compare our packages side-by-side" link).

One of the packages is only for color books and isn't covered here.

The Emerald Package $199 (www.outskirtspress.com/emeraldpublishing.php) includes:

- Choice of two2 full cover templates
- One free author copy
- Interior layout

This package does not include an ISBN, bar code, or any distribution.

The Sapphire Package $399 (www.outskirtspress.com/sapphirepublishing.php) includes:

- Distribution through Ingram, Baker & Taylor, Amazon.com, BarnesandNoble.com, Borders.com, and Booksamillion.com
- 3 copies of the book
- ISBN
- Bar code
- Choice of 9 full color templates

The Ruby Package $599 (www.outskirtspress.com/rubypublishing.php) includes every feature of the Sapphire Package plus:

- Distribution in the UK
- Choice of 16 full color cover templates, instead of 9.
- 6 copies of the book, instead of 3.

The Diamond Package $999 (www.outskirtspress.com/dia-mondpublishing.php) includes every feature of the Ruby Package plus:

- 15 available formats for your book
- 10 free author copies, instead of six6
- 25 customizable cover choices
- Free ebook version

Other than distribution, the only difference among the packages is the author's discount for the purchase of books for resale (25% to 50% discount off the cover price) and a greater profit margin for each book you sell through a third-party retailer. All packages are non-exclusive and the author keeps all rights.

An optional customized cover costs $299.

To make the book available as an ebook, there is an additional cost of $99. However, the ebook is free with the Diamond package.

ROYALTIES PAID TO AUTHOR: Royalties are between 20% and -50% of the net wholesale payment that the Publisher receives from sales, less shipping and handling charges, sales tax charges, and returns or refunds. Authors set the book retail prices, so royalty amounts will vary. You can calculate your royalties at http://outskirtspress.com/calculator.php. For example, for a 230-page book published under the Diamond package, the retail price and royalties could be as follows:

Retail Price	Royalty%	Royalty Amount
$11.95	20%	$2.39
$12.95	25%	$3.24
$13.95	30%	$4.19
$16.95	40%	$6.78

When you click on the "buy now" button on any of the author's pages, you are directed to either Amazon.com, BarnesandNoble.com, or Paypal. Appears that most of the authors' pages go directly to Amazon.com or BarnesandNoble.com. In the above examples, the trade discount is always 20% and according to the calculator, you'd make the royalties (even on sales through Amazon.com, etc.) as set forth above.

Amazon.com charges a 20% trade discount on Outskirts Press books, even though it charges 55% to most other publishers. When pressed for an explanation, Outskirts Press's president, Brent Sampson, stated that its company doesn't have to send books in small orders to Amazon, which would require increased manpower and higher costs on Amazon.com's end. As a result, Amazon.com is willing to take less profit on each sale. According to President Sampson, Outskirts Press uses an inventory management system known as Electronic Data Interchange (EDI), which allows for the transfer of data among different companies using networks and the Internet. When an Amazon.com order is placed for an Outskirts Press book, EDI communicates the order through Outskirts Press's wholesale partners. Turnaround time according to Amazon.com's web site is 24 hours. According to Sampson, EDI drops the discount substantially because "Amazon would rather deal with one wholesaler via EDI handling thousands of books than with thousands of authors via e-mail handling 1 to 2 books. They make their profit in volume, and hence, the considerably lower discount."

NOTABLE PROVISIONS OF THE PUBLISHING CONTRACT: There are four contracts for each of the publishing packages, but they are identical except for the specifics outlined in "Attachment A." The contracts are available at www.outskirtspress. com/Contract_OutskirtsPress.pdf.

The review below covers all four contracts:

Section "I. License" subsection (c) gives the publisher a worldwide, non-exclusive license to print and distribute the work as an ebook or print book.

Section "III. Publisher Services" subsection (a) limits the submission to publication timeline to 90 days, and no more than 180 days.

Outskirts Press was one publisher that took out language regarding ownership of the cover design and formatted book at my request. Now when an author terminates her contract with Outskirts Press she receives all electronic files needed to re-print the book with any other publisher or book printer. It's actions like this that make Outskirts Press a great author-friendly publisher.

Section IV author warranties and Section XII indemnification language are standard and reasonable.

Section XI "Termination" allows either party to cancel the contract on 45 days written notice, which is good. **The last sentence in XI(e) reiterates that the publisher retains all the rights to the layout and cover if either party terminates.**

Section XII subsection (c) contains a clause not often found in such publishing agreements. The publisher does not warrant its services which are provided on an as-is basis. Damages owed to the author are limited to fees "actually paid by the author to the publisher for the one month period prior to publisher's act" that gives rise to the liability. The publisher also isn't liable for any damages that could possibly result from publisher error. This clause probably has little to do with any intentional acts by the publisher, such as refusal to pay royalties or refusal to cease book sales after termination. Don't let this language intimidate you: its bark is worse than its bite.

Section XIII "Force Majeur" means that if the publisher cannot fulfill its obligations under the contract in a timely manner due to reasons out of its control, it is not liable. For example, if a tornado destroys the facility housing the printing press which delays publication of the book within the time required by the contract terms, the publisher is "excused" from the time requirement. This clause is standard in most commercial contracts.

Section XIV "Governing Law" specifies Douglas County, Colorado, as the venue for all legal proceedings.

ALEXA TRAFFIC RANK: 285,182

AUTHOR-FRIENDLY RATING: There is a lot to like. Package fees are generally in the right ballpark, although charges are a bit high for template covers. Outskirts Press incorporates the author's images into the template. However, numerous other self-publishing companies perform the same template cover service but call it "custom", so what you're getting here is really a "custom" cover similar to those provided by other publishers.

Outskirts Press packages' best aspects are the 20% Amazon.com trade discount and the author's purchase price of copies, which is lower than almost any other POD publisher. Both of these aspects alone are reason enough to consider this publisher.

Author web pages have a wonderfully unique feature: the author can easily and frequently update the web page with little programming knowledge. Diamond authors can choose from 16 different web page layouts.

You want a publisher that actually cares if you sell books. For over a year after publication, the publisher's marketing department maintains personal contact with each author and offers marketing guidance and promotional tactics designed to help authors sell books. This guidance includes everything from information about the BXGY program on Amazon.com (how you can list your book on the order page of a book that caters to a similar audience) to editor contact information for magazines such as *Woman's Day* and *Shape*. The author's center makes available contact information for all radio stations and producers in the local area.

This company is impressive and should be on your list of ones to consider.

RJ COMMUNICATIONS
www.selfpublishing.com *or* www.booksjustbooks.com

FORMAT OF BOOKS: Paperback or Hardcover, short run digital or offset printed

GENRES ACCEPTED: All

PUBLISHING FEE: Publisher offers à la carte services. There are no set packages. Services include:

Editorial Analysis—$149 fee which is rebated 100% if additional editorial services are purchased.

Trade Book Editing—$.01 to $.035 per word, depending on complexity.

Children's Book Editing—includes Critique, Text editing, and Illustration editing services by top New York children's book editor.

Text Layout : $250 or more, and author owns the printing file on completion.

Cover and Dust jacket Design —$250 or more, and author owns the printing file on completion.

Bar code—$25

Worldwide Distribution (through Lightning Source service)—$49.95 plus $19.95 per year. This is the database of 26,000 stores, including Amazon.com and BarnesandNoble. com, touted by most PODs. Author earns profits (not royalties) which are paid quarterly for the previous quarter. The only requirement is that the author must purchase at least 100 copies for her own personal inventory.

ISBN: The author purchases the ISBN directly from the US Agency, the only authorized seller of ISBNs. The author, not RJ Communications, is the owner of the ISBN, which is unlike virtually all the other POD practices where the Publisher owns the ISBN.

PROFITS PAID TO AUTHOR: Determined strictly by the author.

For POD books: For example, suppose you sold your 256-page, 5 ½" X 8 ½" book for $14. You would figure a discount of 50% for the retail or wholesale outlet and subtract a printing cost of $.012 per page plus $1 per book for paperback (or $6 per book for hardcover). Your profit per book would be $3.03 per book. A higher retail price yields a higher profit. If you retailed your book for $16, the profit would be $4.03 per book.

For books printed for author distribution: A $100 administrative fee is added to all printing orders. Orders of 100 to 400 copies are printed digitally and orders of 500+ are printed on an offset printing press. For 100 copies of the same 256-page book, the per-book cost would be $5.89. For 500+ copies, the per-book cost would be $5.46, and for 1000+ copies, the per-book cost would be $3.15.

MARKETING PROGRAMS: RJ Communications offers various self-directed marketing programs on an à la carte basis, including online bookstore listing, web site development and design, press release service, and Author Audio Showcase. RJ Communications also offers an ongoing educational program in its *Publishing Basics* programs. Included in the cost of the programs are the books, *Publishing Basics—A Guide for the Small Press and Independent Self-Publisher* and *Publishing Basics for Children's Books*, and the monthly *Publishing Basics newsletter* and *Publishing Basics PodCast*.

NOTABLE PROVISIONS OF THE PUBLISHING AGREEMENT: This isn't a contract as much as it is a purchase order. RJ Communications takes no rights; there is no term clause or any of the other contract provisions you'd normally expect after reading this book. Instead, you execute a purchase order and include the submission checklist found at http://booksjustbooks. com/bookrequest/trade_submission.pdf. If you don't submit the files in perfect condition (for printing), RJ can fix them and charge you for no more than one hour's worth of time, billed at $65. The purchase order and the submission checklist are subject to terms and conditions found at http://booksjustbooks.com/bookrequest/termsandconditions.asp, which are standard and reasonable.

ALEXA TRAFFIC RANK: 139,105

AUTHOR-FRIENDLY RATING: Ron Pramschufer, owner of RJ Communications, is one of the good guys in self-publishing who stands by the idea that anything an author pays to have done remains the property of the author (such as book covers and layout designs). Pramschufer is all about the author and it shows in the pricing. If you want to save money and are okay with the do-it-yourself approach, RJ is the best in the business. RJ is similar to Lulu.com, but probably less well known. Lulu.com was included in this book version because numerous authors contacted me about its services. RJ was included in this version because its service, in most cases, is as good as if not better than Lulu.com. In fact, RJ is more cost effective if you plan on printing more than 20 books.

Pramschufer hosts a radio show on self-publishing and often takes on the giants of the POD industry. He asks questions that need to be asked and demands answers that many self-publishing companies gloss over.

RJ Communications is one of the few companies that are 100% in the author's corner.

TWILIGHT TIMES

www.twilighttimesbooks.com

FORMAT OF BOOKS: ebooks and POD

GENRES ACCEPTED: The publisher seeks creative non-fiction, fantasy, historical, how-to books, humor/satire, juvenile, literary, magic realism, mainstream/contemporary, military/war-related, mystery/suspense, nostalgia-related fiction and non-fiction, paranormal, regional, science fiction, specialty/New Age, supernatural, World War II-related, women's fiction, writing advice, and more. Submission periods vary from six weeks to two months, and you'll need to check the web site to see when submissions are open.

Full submission details are at http://www.twilighttimesbooks.com/subs.html.

PUBLISHING FEES: $0. This publisher is a traditional publisher in every sense, except it offers great royalties. The publisher pays all expenses relating to publication of ebooks or print books, including preview galley copies to reviewers, edits, copy edits, and press releases, as well as formatting, design, artwork, interior layout, and printing. This publisher offers national distribution through Florida Academic Press and Book Clearinghouse.

ROYALTIES PAID TO THE AUTHOR:

- 50% of the retail download price of ebooks sold through the publisher's web site.
- 20% of the retail price of print versions sold through the publisher's web site.
- 50% of the net proceeds of ebooks sold through a third party vendor (Net proceeds equal price of book less the bookseller's discount).
- 15% of the net proceeds of print books sold through a third party vendor like Amazon.com (Net proceeds equal retail price of book less printing cost and the bookseller's discount).

For traditional publishing, these royalties are amazing!

NOTABLE PROVISIONS OF THE PUBLISHING AGREEMENT: The publisher normally provides a sample contract after it receives an author's query letter.

Section I specifies that, in addition to granting print and ebook rights for the term of the contract, the author grants 25% of book club rights, foreign rights, movie rights, television and radio rights, and other such rights.

Normally, this would be a red flag, but because the author can easily get out of this contract, it's less of an issue.

The section restricts authors to selling books on their own at book signings, lectures, promotions, and on consignment to local stores. The author must pay full retail cost for these. When questioned, the publisher reported that it sells books to authors (so that authors can resell at book signings, their own websites, etc.) at wholesale cost. Any author who signs a contract with this publisher should have this section amended to reflect the publisher's actual practice.

Section V calls for a two-year contract term, but publisher Lida Quillen informed me that it would soon change to five years because the publisher fronts all publishing costs, including an initial print run of 300 books. But this section allows the author to terminate the contract with 90 days written notice. Should the author terminate, the publisher retains the right to sell its remaining books (for which the author still receives a royalty).

The publisher shoulders up-front publishing costs and allows an author to terminate at any time; this is something that I've never seen before in the self-publishing industry. Most publishers who front publishing costs NEVER give authors the option to get out so easily. This practice proves that this publisher must not lose many authors and that the authors who publish here are loyal. It speaks volumes.

FREE MARKETING SERVICES OFFERED BY THE PUBLISHER: Here are a few things this publisher does to sell authors books:

- Targeted mailings to several hundred independent bookstores willing to carry books from small press publishers.
- An online media room where members of the media, booksellers and retailers can download flyers, sell sheets, reviews, and chapter excerpts in pdf-formatted files for

print. Makes publisher's catalog available as a download. http://twilighttimesbooks.com/media-room/.

- Media kits and press releases sent to major publications and galleys or advance review copies sent to top reviewers, such as *School Library Journal, American Library Journal, Booklist, Kirkus, Kliatt, Horn Book, NYT Book Review, Publishers Weekly, Washington Post, Boston Globe, Chicago-Sun Times, WSJ, Oregonian,* and *Seattle Times.*
- Delivery of promotional packets to the Community Relations Managers of the Barnes & Noble bookstores in regions where author resides.
- Delivery of postcards, flyers, and brochures to targeted independent booksellers, specialty shops, and book catalogs. Delivery of press releases and news stories to the author's local and regional newspapers, libraries, bookstores, and associations. Online posting of news stories and articles on newsgroups, readers' bulletin boards, and readers' e-mail lists.

ALEXA TRAFFIC RANK: 1,423,411

AUTHOR-FRIENDLY RATING: One of the truly great opportunities for new authors. The publisher fronts all publishing costs and allows the author to terminate the contract with 90 days written notice. The publisher aggressively markets its authors' books.

Unlike most publishers covered here, Twilight Times selectively chooses what it publishes. If you're fortunate enough to be considered for publication, you'd be crazy not to accept a contract.

VIRTUAL BOOKWORM
www.virtualbookworm.com

FORMAT OF BOOKS: ebook, paperback, and hardback

GENRES ACCEPTED: All, except those which deal with New Age, the occult, or eroticism, or which promote hate or violence.

PUBLISHING FEE:

$99 for ebook (lowered to $65 if purchased with a print package) (www.virtualbookworm.com/ebookpublishing.html).

$360–$1,950 for a paperback print package. Details at www.virtualbookworm.com/podsoftcover.html.

$430–$2,100 for a hardcover print package. Details at www.virtualbookworm.com/podhardcover.html

$590–$2,225 for a combo hardcover and paperback package. Details at www.virtualbookworm.com/podcombo.html

All POD packages include:
- Choice of 5"x 8", 5.25"x 8", 6"x 9", or 8.25"x 11" trim size with full-color cover
- Basic cover design
- Electronic proof
- ISBN assignment (for the printed version)
- Copyright application kit
- Book page on publisher's web site
- Bar code
- 15 internal graphics or images (must be submitted to specs)
- Data Backup
- Full Distribution
- Drop Shipment
- Book registration through Amazon.com, Books In Print, and Borders
- 50% royalties of net receipts (Approximately 30–35% of cover price on books sold through publisher)
- Author may purchase first order of book for 50% off list

price (subsequent orders 30% off, and discount increases with larger orders)

More expensive packages include:

- LCCN
- Professional cover
- Professional editing

Like many PODs today, Virtual Bookworm offers a Returns and Bookstore Rep program which entices traditional booksellers to carry your book. The cost to enroll is $500 for the first year and $140 for all subsequent years (www.virtualbookworm.com/return-program.html).

ROYALTIES PAID TO AUTHOR: For print books: 50% of the Net Publisher Receipts, which is the book price less credit card charges, shipping and handling charges, charge backs, discounts, or disputes. A complete explanation is available at www.book-wormpublishing.com/supportcenter/kb.cgi?view=26&lang=en. Author also receives 50% of Net Publisher Print Receipts for books the author permits the publisher to sell through third parties. For details on print royalties, see Paragraph 6 of the Print on Demand Publishing Agreement.

For ebooks: 50% of the Net Publisher Print Receipts, which is the book price less credit card fees, shipping and handling charges, or disputes. For details on ebook royalties, see Paragraph 7 of the Electronic Publishing Agreement.

All royalties are paid monthly so long as they exceed $25; otherwise, they are held until royalties reach $25.

NOTABLE PROVISIONS OF THE PUBLISHING AGREEMENTS: There are two publishing agreements, one for POD and one for epublishing. The POD contract is at http://www.virtualbookworm.com/infodocs/2005podcontract.pdf, and the epublishing contract is at http://www.virtualbookworm.com/infodocs/2005ebookcontract.pdf.

Most agreements are nearly identical. Unless otherwise noted, the provisions discussed are in both agreements.

The introductory portion sets the contract term to two years, beginning on the date the contract is signed. It also states that the contract is exclusive.

Paragraph 1 allows the publisher to seek injunctive relief if the author enters into another agreement prior to contract termination which conflicts with the publisher's rights. Injunctive relief as a remedy allows the publisher to impose a court order which forces the author to stop selling the book elsewhere. The author also agrees to pay the publisher's legal fees and court costs.

This provision gives the publisher the upper hand because if a dispute arises, and the author decides to publish elsewhere, the author subjects himself to the publisher's whims. The author could end up shouldering hefty attorneys' fees, including those charged by the publisher's attorneys. The fees could greatly outweigh the actual loss of revenue and far exceed any royalties, whether actual or potential. The more reasonably drafted attorneys' fees clause directs the losing party to pay the winning party's fees. It keeps everyone honest.

If you enter a publishing agreement with this publisher, insist that the last sentence in Paragraph 1 be changed from:

> "Author will also reimburse VirtualBookworm.
> com Publishing Inc. for all court costs and legal
> fees incurred,"

to:

> "Author will also reimburse Virtualbookworm
> Publishing, Inc. for all court costs and legal fees
> incurred, only if Virtualbookworm's claims against
> the author are upheld by a court; otherwise, Vir-
> tualbookworm will reimburse the author for all
> his/her court costs and legal fees."

The bottom line: avoid breaching the contract when termination by the author is so easy.

Paragraph 3 allows either party to terminate the contract with 90 days written notice. There is a $50 fee if the author terminates prior to the expiration of the two-year term. No big deal. That's fair.

Paragraph 5 of the POD Publishing Agreement allows the author to search for a traditional publisher that will print at least 1,000 copies of the author's book in the first printing. Other than that exception, this paragraph prohibits the author from contracting with another POD publisher during the term of the contract (which remember can be canceled with 90 days notice). This clause protects the author who has an opportunity to sign with a traditional publisher, but who hasn't given the 90 days notice of termination. So, if Random House wants to sign you, you can do so before formally terminating the agreement.

Paragraph 5 of the Electronic Publishing Agreement prohibits the sale of the author's ebook on the author's web site, unless it is linked to the sales page on Virtualbookworm. This prevents the author from cutting out the publisher and making 100% of the royalties from each book sale.

ADDITIONAL SERVICES: A complete description of additional services can be found at www.virtualbookworm.com/additionalservices.html, so I will only mention the highlights.

The publisher offers marketing and promotional services.

At $95, the professional cover isn't a bad deal, but request a sample, as this is an extremely low price.

At $75, the publisher places your book in *Ingram's Advance Magazine*. This price is fair, since most PODs charge more.

Before paying for a marketing package, find out if the 200 media outlets which will receive your press release are the same regardless of the type of book. My guess is that the same 200 media outlets receive a press release whether the book is a vampire novel or a true account of child abuse. Also, check with the publisher and find out which "10 major reviewers" receive a copy of your book.

ALEXA TRAFFIC RANK: 646,259

AUTHOR-FRIENDLY RATING: Overall, depending on what package you choose, this can be a good deal. The $99 ebook package is not worth it, especially since there are many publishers who will charge nothing to put your ebook up for sale. If you add a professional cover and ebook publication to the basic package, it jumps from $360 to $520, which is still a good price.

The royalties are acceptable. You won't find many higher offers elsewhere, especially from PODs. Payments of 50% of net royalties actually turn out to be between 30% and 35% of the retail price of the books sold through the publisher's own bookstore. Ebook royalties are closer to an actual 50%. This publisher deducts credit card processing fees before calculating the royalty percentage, while some other publishers include credit card fees in their calculations, but this is minor.

The $790 package is probably the best overall deal and the cheapest publishing package with editing services. It includes professional editing of up to 75,000 words.

The retail price of the books is excellent. A 432-page, paperback book sells for $16.95, which is great. The publisher charges the author 50% of the cover price on the first order of paperback books, but the discount on subsequent orders is 30%. For hardcovers, the author receives 35% off the cover price on the first order, and 30% off on subsequent orders. But publisher Bobby Bernshausen states, "If an author is trying to get the books into bookstores, we work to get the discount high enough for placement."

On the negative side, the author must pay $50 for early contract termination, and the attorneys' fees clause is one sided.

Nevertheless, this publisher has a long history and a solid reputation. The negatives aren't deal-breakers, and should be negotiated. I like this publisher.

WASTELAND PRESS
www.wastelandpress.net

FORMAT OF BOOKS: POD paperbacks, hardbacks, and ebooks

GENRES ACCEPTED: fiction, poetry, and short stories

PUBLISHING FEES:

Ebook Publishing $75 and includes:

- Full color cover design
- Light editing, including spell check (two hours total)
- Sold via publisher's online bookstore
- 25% royalty
- Option to later convert to paperback publishing at half the retail price

(www.wastelandpress.net/Ebooks.html)

The prices of the print packages depend on length of the book. The cost of each package below is based on a book between 176 and 225 pages (prices are higher for books above 225 pages)

Basic Plan $195 (http://www.wastelandpress.net/Basicplan.html) (for 20- to 300-page book) and includes:

- 5 copies in paperback
- Full color cover design
- Basic distribution (Amazon.com, BarnesandNoble.com)
- 10% royalty
- ISBN, barcode (additional $50)

Silver Plan $440 (http://www.wastelandpress.net/Silverplan.html) and includes:

- 25 paperback copies of book
- Full color cover design
- Basic distribution (Amazon.com, BarnesandNoble.com)
- ISBN, Bar code
- 20% royalty

Gold Plan $925 (http://www.wastelandpress.net/Goldplan. html) and includes:

- 100 paperback copies of your book
- Full-color cover design
- ISBN, Bar code
- Full-service marketing (5 books sent for reviews from various publications; placement on Amazon.com and BarnesandNoble.com via Ingram distribution; marketing to libraries, and placement in Ingram Advance Catalog for additional $100. For complete marketing details go to www.wastelandpress.net/Marketing.html)
- 25% royalty

Platinum Plan $1,440 ((http://www.wastelandpress.net/Platinumplan.html) includes every feature in Gold Plan PLUS:

- 10 books sent for reviews with various publications, instead of 5 books sent to reviewers.
- 175 paperback copies of your book, instead of 100 copies of your book.
- 30% royalty

Titanium Plan $1,650 (http://www.wastelandpress.net/Titaniumplan.html) and includes every feature in Platinum Plan PLUS:

- Hardback publication
- 10 hardback copies of your book
- 15 books sent for reviews with various publications, instead of 10 in the Platinum plan.

Complete details of the publishing packages can be found at www.wastelandpress.net/Spublishing.html.

ROYALTIES PAID TO AUTHOR: Because the author sets the book price, the author determines royalties. An author who has a standard 230-page paperback can retail the book between $8.95 and $19.95. The author's royalty is between 10%-30% of the retail price less any discounts given to third party vendors.

That author can also purchase up to 100 book copies for 50% of the retail price (100+ copies are 60% off). So, depending on your book price, you can purchase copies and make a respectable profit through resales.

NOTABLE PROVISIONS OF THE PUBLISHING AGREEMENT: Links to the publishing agreements can be found at: http://www.wastelandpress.net/Pubagreements.html

Provisions in the various contracts are the same, except for royalty percentages. Although the author can cancel at any time without notice, the author is responsible for the publisher's costs incurred through the termination date if termination occurs prior to publication.

ALEXA TRAFFIC RANK: 1,636,708

AUTHOR-FRIENDLY RATING: Wasteland Press is a shining example of why smaller is often better. The hands-on assistance and meticulous care to each publishing project is a huge plus. The packages are priced fabulously; it's difficult to see how this publisher makes any profit.

The author can choose a basic package and upgrade at any time by paying the difference. This flexibility is advantageous if book sales increase because an upgrade allows the author to increase the royalty percent and receive additional books for resale.

The publisher's statement in its FAQs (http://www.wastelandpress.net/Faq2.html) sums up its approach: "[I]t is our job to market your book in order to make money . . . We have to make money from your book, not from you!"

The above statement is why Wasteland Press is ranked as one of the top publishers in this book.

WRITERS EXCHANGE E-PUBLISHING INTERNATIONAL

www.writers-exchange.com/epublishing/submission.htm

FORMAT OF BOOK: ebooks and paperback

GENRES ACCEPTED: A variety of fiction and nonfiction. A complete list is at www.writers-exchange.com/epublishing/submission.htm.

PUBLISHING FEES: $0 for ebooks; $99 for POD (the publisher uses Booksurge, and appears just to pass the set-up fee on to the author).

There are two publishing programs detailed at www.writers-exchange.com/epublishing/submission.htm.

Distribution Program sells your completed, edited, and formatted book with its own cover on a non-exclusive basis. Provides no promotion.

Publication Program is similar to a traditional publisher's agreement. The publisher provides editing, cover art, and promotion for the book. Promotion entails sending the book to three reviewers minimum, nominating it for awards, and listing or selling it on affiliated web sites. This is an exclusive contract.

The publisher's comments about the program differences follow:

"1. If you are 'published' by Writers Exchange (exclusive contract) then together with the Author, we are responsible for any errors in the book. If you find a mistake three years after the book is released, we will still fix the error and send out new copies of the books.

2. We also send the book out to reviewers and nominate the books for awards. Book reviews are an ongoing process and is not limited to the time that the book is first released.

3. We list your books at distribution web sites and ebook lists—giving more exposure to your work.

4. Any promotional activities we undertake are generally only extended to the published books (obviously more people coming to the web site helps distributed authors too, but not to the same extent).

5. Only published books are eligible to be made into any new formats that come along. At the moment all published books are available in pdf, rtf, html, (if the book suits these formats). Writers Exchange E-Publishing formats the books for the authors.

6. Only those exclusive contracts are sent to conversion web sites—ie. all 'published' books are soon to be released at pdastore.com in hand-held format.

7. Only those authors with exclusive contracts are consulted about the happenings at Writers Exchange E-Publishing. Often authors are asked to vote on how they would like certain issues handled (which then becomes company policy). This is only extended to those with exclusive contracts—we consider the 'published' authors part of the family and they have a voice in the business.

   Non-Exclusive contracts allow the author to list their books wherever they please (provided the place accepts non-exclusive agreements). So Writers Exchange E-Publishing is just another outlet for their sales. There is no 'loyalty' to Writers Exchange required, which differentiates the non-exclusive and exclusive contract mindset."

ROYALTIES PAID TO THE AUTHOR:

Ebooks

60% of the retail download price if submitted with cover art;
50% of the retail download price if publisher provides cover art; or
40% of the retail download price on illustrated books.

Print books

The author receives 60% of the retail price less production costs ($5.00) and credit card processing fees. POD books sell for $9.95. The cost to produce the book is $5, which leaves $4.95 (less credit card processing fees) to divide 60/40 between the author and the publisher.

NOTABLE PROVISIONS OF THE PUBLISHING AGREEMENT: Their Exclusive Publishing Agreement and the Distribution Agreement can be found at www.writers-exchange. com/epublishing/submission.htm.

The Exclusive Publishing Agreement

Paragraph 2 gives the publisher the exclusive right to publish and sell the book in digital format only, such as electronic download, CD, or disk. The contract does not mention exclusive rights for print books. Because courts generally construe contract language in the author's favor, this lack of mention probably doesn't harm the author. The writer can also cancel the contract with 90 days notice, so there's no reason for the author to bring up this point during negotiations.

Paragraph 7 sets no time limit on the contract term, and specifies that the contract remains in force until one party provides 90 days written notice via certified mail.

Paragraph 9 requires the author to provide a link to the publisher's web site if the author includes an excerpt from the book on his web site.

Paragraph 10 prohibits the author from selling the book to a third party once the publisher edits or makes changes to the work. This restriction applies even after the contract terminates. There is no way they could stop you from selling a version that is similar to their edited version, since once you see the edited version, you may need to make the same edits to the original that they have (spelling, grammar, etc.)

The Distribution Agreement

Paragraph 2 only grants non-exclusive electronic rights in English to the publisher.

Paragraph 3 includes the author's warranty that the submitted material doesn't infringe on anyone's copyright or other rights.

Paragraphs 4 and 5 permit the publisher to use the author's name and likeness on the publisher's web site to promote the work.

Paragraph 7 permits either party to terminate the agreement with 90 days written notice.

The Distribution Agreement lacks a statement covering royalties. The author should request written confirmation from the publisher that royalty amounts are the same as those specified in Paragraphs 8 and 13 of the Exclusive Publishing Agreement.

The Standard Artist Agreement

This agreement should be signed by the parties if the publisher finds a cover artist to create the book cover or illustrations.

Paragraph 4 specifies that if the author uses the cover artist's artwork on any other item besides the book, the cover artist is entitled to 50% of the net profits. For example, if the author sells coasters imposed with an image of the book cover, the cover artist receives 50% of what the author makes from coaster sales.

Paragraph 2, Section 2, requires the author to provide royalty statements to the artist. This is confusing because the publisher submits payments directly to the artist. This section requires clarification.

Section 3 requires the author to pay the cover artist the difference between the base fees listed here less any royalties already paid in the event the author terminates the agreement before the artist has earned $50 in royalties from the creation of cover art or $200 in royalties from the creations of illustrations. According to Section 5, the author's payment is not for ownership in the cover art or illustrations. Such payment doesn't give the author ownership in the cover art and/or illustrations.

ALEXA TRAFFIC RANK: 874,173

AUTHOR-FRIENDLY RATING: This publisher makes its money from sales of the author's work, not from the author. This is the type of company an author wants for a publisher.

The publisher actively promotes the author's work by sending out review copies, nominating its authors for awards, selling books through book distributions sites, and engaging in other related promotional activities.

This publisher doesn't publish everything that comes along, but chooses books it believes will sell.

If the publisher chooses an author's book, the publisher pays for cover art, editing, and any other expense (except for the POD $99 printer set-up fee). In exchange, the author gives the publisher exclusive rights, but can always terminate with 90 days written notice.

The royalty structure is as generous as any other publisher. U.S. writers should be aware that the publisher is located in Australia.

This one's a winner regardless of which continent you're on.

XULON PRESS
www.xulonpress.com

FORMAT OF BOOK: paperback and hardback

GENRES ACCEPTED: Christian books only; books must support core Christian beliefs and values. Many categories, including Christian living, theology, church growth, discipleship, Bible study, fiction, poetry, and biographies.

PUBLISHING FEES: $1,499 package includes:

- Custom book cover
- Professionally formatted text
- ISBN, Bar Code, and listing in Books-In-Print
- 100% royalty rate on all trade sales
- 10 free copies
- Author discounts up to 70% off the retail price
- Personal web page from online bookstore
- Order/Pak & Ship Service offered 24 hours a day, 7 days a week (toll-free order service takes phone orders and ships books to customers)
- Distribution to major book distributors and 25,000 bookstores, including 2,500 Christian bookstores
- Internet promotion on Amazon.com, Target.com, Borders.com, and BarnesandNoble.com
- Marketing to 1,000s of Christian bookstores and 1,000 leading churches in the publisher's catalog, *Christian Book Browser*
- Promotion at the International Christian Retail Show twice a year with catalogs and multimedia presentations
- Notification to 3,000 Christian broadcasters and journalists through Xulon's Christian Media Alert publication

Complete information on the publishing package is at www.xulonpress.com/book-publishing.htm.

ROYALTIES PAID TO AUTHOR: 100% net receipts from all sales to bookstores (the retail price less the bookseller discount and the cost to print). For books sold directly from Xulon, the author receives 75% of full retail price less the actual costs to print the book. To learn more about how royalties are calculated go to http://www.xulonpress.com/royalties-discounts.htm.

PURCHASE PRICE OF THE BOOKS: Determined by book's page count. A complete pricing chart is at http://www.xulonpress.com/christian-book-publisher-faqs.htm#Who%20determines%20the%20retail%20price%20of%20my%20book?.

NOTABLE PROVISIONS OF THE PUBLISHING AGREEMENT: The publishing agreement is at https://secure11.hostek.net/secure1/xulonpress/xulon-publishing-agreement.htm (go to Step 4).

"Author Right to Ownership" and "Author Right to Copyright" establish that the author holds complete control of the work at all times, and can sell it to a third party at any time.

"Term and Termination" specifies that the author determines the term of the agreement.

"Cover Design" specifies that the author receives an original cover using stock photos or images which author submits, but the author does not receive the original artwork.

"Miscellaneous Fees" imposes charges on the author for work which requires editing. The author may receive 10 minor edit changes for free. After 10 changes, the publisher charges $50 plus $2 for each minor change.

ALEXA TRAFFIC RANK: 250,769

AUTHOR-FRIENDLY RATING: The publisher offers a non-exclusive contract and competitive pricing at the retail level. The royalties are fantastic, and the author purchases copies with excellent pricing.

The marketing services included in the package justify the publisher's additional fees. There is no better self-publishing company around for authors targeting the Christian market.

The publisher is a member of Christian Booksellers Association and Evangelical Christian Publishers Association, associations that may provide additional information and references.

CHAPTER 7

Some Pretty Good Self-Publishing Companies

How do you separate an outstanding publisher from a pretty good one? By examining factors such as the publisher's pricing, the author's royalties, and the publisher's contract. Publishers that earned a pretty good rating typically exhibited one aspect that was unfavorable to authors, such as low royalties or a clause in their contract that wasn't author-friendly which the publisher would not change.

The publishers in this section are good companies and provide an excellent service. Read their reviews, and if the deficiencies don't bother you, then publish your work through one of them. These companies all provide solid services.

In fact, many pretty good publishers are one mere tweak away from the outstanding category. With one change in the contract, higher royalties, or lower retail costs, a publisher could jump to the next level. That's how close many of them are to being outstanding.

AVENTINE PRESS

www.aventinepress.com

FORMAT OF BOOKS: paperback and hardcover

GENRES ACCEPTED: All

PUBLISHING FEES: $349 package (www.aventinepress. com/services.html) includes:

- Generic cover design (created from template)
- Choice of interior style templates
- ISBN
- Author's bio and photo, and cover photos or graphics supplied by author included in the book and on the cover
- Electronic proof of the book
- UPC bar code
- Listing with online booksellers
- Book and cover on a CD

Go to www.aventinepress.com/services.html for more details on the publishing programs.

PRICE OF BOOKS: Based on the finished page count (.0154 x # of pages + .90 for cover of paperback or $7.55 for cover of hard back). See www.aventinepress.com/pub_agree.html.

108- to 200-page paperback retails for $10.95 to $12.95.
201- to 300-page paperback retails for $13.95 to $16.95.
301- to 400-page paperback retails for $17.95 to $20.95.

ROYALTIES PAID TO AUTHOR: 80% of the "Net Amount" received from each book sale. "Net Amount" is the cover price less trade discount less single copy printing cost.

All books are sold through third party retailers. The publisher's web site gives this example: if a 160-page book has a cover price of $12.95, the trade discount an online book retailer is 55%, or $7.12 per book, and the single copy printing cost is $3.30. This leaves a Net Amount of $2.53. The author receives 80% of $2.53, which is $2.02.

NOTABLE PROVISIONS OF THE PUBLISHING AGREEMENT: The contract is available at www.aventinepress. com/pub_agree.html. The publisher uses a straightforward contract.

"Warranties Section" is standard and reasonable.

"The Rights to Your Own Work" makes it clear that the publisher claims no right to your work. The author also acknowledges that the publisher has no responsibility to correct or review the work prior to publication.

"Indemnities" says that, if warranties made by the author are false, the author is financially liable for any losses sustained by the publisher as a result of a lawsuit, including legal fees. This is fair: if an author lies about ownership of the work or even assumes she's can use some material without checking to see if it's copyrighted and the publisher is sued by the actual owner because of it, the author should have to pay the publisher's legal fees.

"Terms and Exclusivity" is as author-friendly as they come: it's non-exclusive so the author can enter into other publishing agreements. This section also describes the publishing fee portion which will be refunded to the author depending on specific circumstances.

"Complete Agreement" voids any and all promises made prior to the signing of the contract which fail to appear in the contract.

"Law & Venue" requires arbitration for all monetary disputes. This requirement doesn't preclude equitable relief, such as a court order prohibiting the publisher from distributing the book after termination of the contract. Court action must be brought in California, but the contract doesn't necessarily require arbitration hearings to be held in California. This evens the playing field when a dispute arises, since an author won't have to travel to California to arbitrate. When a contract doesn't state where arbitration must occur, it can be done either by phone or somewhere convenient to both parties.

OTHER SERVICES OFFERED: View all optional services at www.aventinepress.com/services.html.

$250 for custom cover design
$.015 per word for copy editing
$995 for the publisher's marketing program, detailed at
www.aventinepress.com/market.html.

Registering the book at the U.S. Copyright Office and submitting it to Bowker's Books In Print are important, but purchasing these services on your own costs much less. This program isn't good value.

ALEXA TRAFFIC RANK: 1,001,974

AUTHOR-FRIENDLY RATING: This company could serve authors better if it offered direct sales on its web site. The 80% royalty is great. Overall, this is a good deal.

BOOKSURGE PUBLISHING
www.booksurgepublishing.com

FORMAT OF BOOKS: paperbacks hardcovers, and ebooks

GENRES ACCEPTED: All

PUBLISHING FEES: Offers several publishing programs and provides an overview at www.booksurgepublishing.com/programs.php.

$498 Author's Advantage Publishing Program is the most popular. It's discussed in detail at www.booksurgepublishing.com/ppadvantage.php, and includes:

- Publisher's cover and background templates (author creates cover and provides graphics for templates)

- Complete book formatting and page layout
- ISBN
- Listing the book on the publisher's online store

ROYALTIES PAID TO AUTHOR:

25% of the retail sales price for paperbacks
15% of the retail sales price for hardcovers
70% of the retail sales price for ebooks
10% on bookstore orders

NOTABLE PROVISIONS OF THE AUTHOR AGREE-MENT: View the contract at http://booksurgepublishing.com/images/downloads/Author_Publishing_Agreement.pdf.

This is an excellent contract for authors.

In "License to Publish," the author gives the publisher a non-exclusive license to publish the book during the contract term.

"Term" makes it clear that the contract term lasts until the author terminates with 30 days written notice or via e-mail.

"General Provisions" could cause a problem for the author. It states, "This Agreement may be modified by the PUBLISHER giving 30 days notice to the AUTHOR of the proposed change." If the author disagrees with the change, the author must promptly terminate the contract. For example, if Booksurge decides to change author royalties from 25% to 20%, the author must cancel the contract before the change goes into effect. Otherwise, the author is deemed to have agreed to the modification. Of course, you can always terminate later by giving 30 days notice. However, if the publisher decides to change the contract, and give itself exclusive worldwide rights for X years and prohibit the author from terminating the contract until that period is over, the author could be stuck if he fails to cancel the contract before the change goes into effect.

AUTHORS DISCOUNT ON BOOKS: Because Booksurge is a complete à la carte service, the author's success depends on driving potential buyers to the online bookstore and the author's personal sales of the book. The minimum retail price for a 201- to 250-page, 5.25" x 8" paperback book is $13.99. The discount off this retail price to authors depends on volume:

```
1–9 books  . . . . . . . . . 30%
10–50 books  . . . . . . . 35%
51–99 books. . . . . . . . 40%
100–249 books  . . . . . 50%
250–499 books. . . . . . 60%
500–999 books. . . . . . 65%
1000+. . . . . . . . . . . . . 70%
```

Booksurge offers excellent pricing because it keeps its printing in-house, unlike many PODs publishers. In fact, Booksurge does the printing for many PODs. If you want to sell books from your own web site and purchase them in quantities of 100 from Booksurge, you could sell your book for $10 to $11, which is reasonable for a paperback by an unknown writer, and still make a nice profit.

ALEXA TRAFFIC RANK: 85,217

AUTHOR-FRIENDLY RATING: Booksurge gets a 10 for its contract, but a 2 for its up-front fees. For $498, your package should include a customized cover, placement on Amazon.com, and more. Instead, you create a cover from templates, and still must supply your own graphics and pay an additional $50 to list on Amazon.com (www.booksurgepublishing.com/amazon.php).

If the initial package was $200 less, I'd rave about Booksurge. This company only makes sense if you plan to make most book sales on your own.

Booksurge's primary business model focuses on selling book publishing packages to authors rather than on driving potential readers to its online bookstore. Unless you are market savvy, you will flounder. If you want complete control of your book sales, Booksurge's wholesale pricing makes your own sales more profitable.

Your publishing experience with Booksurge will likely be satisfactory, but until Booksurge takes advantage of its relationship with Amazon.com and lists its authors on Amazon.com, it remains a just pretty good publisher.

EBOOKSTAND

www.ebookstand.com

FORMAT OF BOOKS: ebook and POD

GENRES ACCEPTED: All

PUBLISHING FEES: Prices vary depending on whether books are paperback or hardcover. A full pricing description is available at www.ebookstand.com/pricing.htm. Publishing package prices for a standard 5.25" x 8.25" paperback are:

$449 for a 25- to 100-page book
$559 for a 101- to 200-page book
$649 for a 201- to 300-page book
$749 for a 301- to 400-page book
$849 for a 401- to 500-page book.

This package includes:
- 52 copies
- Unlimited photos, tables, and charts

- ISBN
- Bar code
- Books In Print registration
- e-Commerce web page for your book
- Electronic proof
- Printed proof
- PDF ebook available for sale
- Cover art (additional $300)

SELLING PRICE OF YOUR BOOK: For ebooks, the publisher suggests a price of less than $10, but the author sets the final price. For paperbacks, selling price depends on the page count: 101 to 200 pages sells for $15.95; 201 to 300 pages sells for $18.95; and 301 to 400 pages sells for $22.95.

ROYALTIES PAID TO AUTHOR: 50% of the purchase price of an ebook, 30% of the purchase price of each paperback sold through Ebookstand, and 15% of the retail price of books sold through third party retailers (e.g. Amazon.com).

NOTABLE PROVISIONS OF THE PUBLISHING AGREEMENT: The complete contract is at www.ebookstand. com/register.htm.

The author grants non-exclusive rights to the publisher, and can terminate at any time.

Unless author purchases the publisher's editing services, the publisher provides no editing whatsoever.

If the author terminates the contract after acceptance but prior to fulfillment, the publisher returns the fee less a $75 processing charge.

If the author's book makes no sales after 18 months, the publisher may remove the book from its web site.

TIME FROM SUBMISSION TO PUBLICATION: Ebook takes 5 to 10 days. Print book takes about one month.

OTHER SERVICES AVAILABLE:

$75 Publisher archives your book on CD-Rom

$275 Text editing services for up to 80,000 words

Offers a Bookmarket Map, which is a directory of publishers containing thousands of potential buyers.

ALEXA TRAFFIC RANK: 512,188

AUTHOR-FRIENDLY RATING: All potential authors receive a book, *The Self Publishing Checklist*, from the company's CEO. The book is filled with useful information.

Authors receive exceptional value on publishing packages. You receive 52 copies of your book. Even though a custom cover isn't included in the price, $300 for a custom cover isn't unreasonable.

The contract itself is excellent: the non-exclusivity and royalties are author-friendly. It's the publishing fees and the prices at which the paperback version of your book must retail that makes it tough to recommend this publisher.

Authors can purchase copies for their resales at a reasonable price. For a 230-page book, an author pays $6.85 when ordering 25 or more. Price breaks increase for larger orders.

The only downside here is the book's retail price. At $18.95 for a 230-page book, which is $2-$3 higher than comparable books, the book may prove more difficult to sell. The high retail price is the only thing keeping this publisher from being one of the best.

ECHELON PRESS
www.echelonpress.com

FORMAT OF BOOKS: ebook and paperback

GENRES ACCEPTED: Novels in these genres: Adventure/Thriller, Historical Western, Horror, Young Adult, Historical Romance, Ultra-Sensual Romance. The work must be between 50,000 and 120,000 words. You must check the submissions periods on the website (http://www.echelonpress.com/submission.htm) to determine when this publisher is accepting manuscripts.

PUBLISHING FEES: $0. Like a traditional publisher, Echelon Press provides editing, cover art, and promotion (www.echelonpress.com/authorfaq.htm).

ROYALTIES PAID TO THE AUTHOR:

50% for ebooks downloaded from the publisher's web site

10% for paperbacks

NOTABLE PROVISIONS OF THE PUBLISHING AGREEMENT: The contract is unavailable on the publisher's web site, but owner Karen Syed provided a copy upon request.

Below are the relevant sections of the contract:

"Grant of Rights" gives the publisher two-year exclusive rights to publish the book in print and electronic form. The author keeps movie, television, and similar rights.

Since Echelon Press is really a traditional publisher (edits and markets the books without charging fees to the author), this is reasonable. Syed explained her company's two-year exclusive rights policy:

> "Our 'two-years from actual date of publication' item is what makes us stand out from other publishers. We aren't in it just to publish anyone who wants it. We have really tightened our belt on the level of writing we require, the quality of our covers, and we are not like the subsidy pubs who authors can pay and have it their way. We are a traditional publisher that pays royalties, helps in

marketing, offers standard retail/distribution discounts appropriately and offer retailers full return ability. We are working on distribution venues that will get our titles on the shelf. So you see, we are a publisher for the long haul not just to allow authors to be published.

We do a lot for the authors, as much if not more than most houses. Fabulous cover art, full editing (we are focusing very strongly on this now), marketing to stores, distributors, libraries, and anywhere else we can. We co-sponsor cooperative event programs that allows authors to network and reach readers in the public forum for a minimal cost. Our books and/or authors have been showcased at BEA, ALA, Printer's Row, we are going to be at the Southern Festival of Books, Amelia Book Island Festival and numerous others."

"Author's Copies" gives the author 10 free paperback copies and 40% off the cover price for additional copies to be used at author appearances for resale, which enables the author to make more money from personal sales without sharing proceeds with the publisher.

"Royalties On Publisher Editions" contains author royalty percentages mentioned earlier. Echelon Press incurs a lot of expenses to cover editing, book cover design, and marketing, so the author royalty amounts are fair. Royalties are calculated on the Net, and the contract defines how the Net is calculated. Many PODs that pay a much higher royalty on print books do not offer editing, marketing, and promotions at no additional charge to the author.

"Subsidiary and Secondary Rights" assigns all other rights, except print and electronic, to the author. Syed explained that this section mainly refers to Book Club sales.

"Author's Non-Competition Clause" allows an author, who first published a political thriller about American politics with

Echelon, to publish another similarly themed book with a different publisher during the term. The author cannot publish a book that is basically the same story as the one under contract with identical or nearly identical characters. Thus, you can't get around this contract by republishing a similar version of your book with another POD publisher. Any book that directly competes with the publisher's book under contract violates this clause.

"Reversion of Rights" is flexible. The author may terminate the contract by paying a $250 termination fee and the "outstanding financial obligations" relating to production, which are probably negligible and should be verified by the author by requesting to review the publisher's records. The cost to an author for early termination allows the author to respond to a big-time publisher who expresses interest in the book.

Arbitration proceedings take place in Forth Worth, Texas, and the loser pays the winner's attorneys' fees, which is standard in many business contracts.

When viewed as a whole, this contract is fair. It is longer than most other publishers' contracts and, like any well-written commercial contract (meaning it was written by a lawyer), there is little wiggle room. If an author elects to sign the contract without consulting a lawyer, he cannot later use his lack of representation as an excuse to escape contract obligations.

ALEXA TRAFFIC RANK: No Data

AUTHOR-FRIENDLY RATING: If you dream about signing with the big boys, Echelon Press is a good warm up because its publishing process closely mirrors traditional publishing. Echelon Press takes your book through professional editing and marketing. The $250 buyout clause is reasonable and the contract is the real deal, so understand every detail before you sign.

The only negative is that 10% royalty on paperbacks is low for PODs, but again, Echelon Press is really a traditional publisher.

FOREMOST PRESS
(formerly Action Tales)
www.foremostpress.com

FORMAT OF BOOK: ebook and paperback

GENRES ACCEPTED: Novels of 50,000 or more words. Authors must make a sales pitch to the publisher, who makes a decision based on author's writing quality, the characters, the pace of the book, and the plot.

Go to http://www.foremostpress.com/authors/ for complete guideline information.

PUBLISHING FEES: The two publishing programs are:

Plan A—$347, includes:

- Light edit
- ISBN
- 10 copies of the book
- PDF version of book for ebook sales
- 4 page web site with a sales page on publisher's web site
- Listing on Amazon, BarnesandNoble.com, and Baker & Taylor
- Customized typesetting

Plan B—$197, includes everything in Plan A except customized typesetting.

Neither package includes a cover, which costs an additional $150 unless author supplies the cover.

ROYALTIES PAID TO AUTHOR:

Ebooks Transaction fee of $.97 to the publisher.

The publisher and author then split the sales price 50/50. The author sets the sales price, although publisher suggests a maximum $6.97, which would give author $3.00 per sale.

Paperbacks For retail sales on the publisher's web site, author receives 20% of the gross sales price. For wholesales, the publisher and author split the difference between the cost and price. Foremost Press provides this example: if a 200- to 236-page book lists at $13.97, the author's 20% royalty is $2.74. For sales through third party retailers and bookstores, the author receives 10% of the wholesale price.

To figure out the pricing for your book, go to: http://www.foremostpress.com/authors/#pricebook.
Authors can purchase copies for 50% of the retail price. This pricing is excellent!

NOTABLE PROVISIONS OF THE PUBLISHING AGREEMENT: The contract is at http://foremostpress.com/authors/agreement.html.

If there is a Comeback Publisher of the Year Award for author-friendly contracts, Foremost Press wins hands down. The publisher replaced the terrible Action Tales contract with the shortest publishing contract I've ever seen.

The contract condenses what most 10-page publishing contracts say into one. It sets forth royalty rights, and allows either party to cancel at any time by giving 120 days e-mail notice. The author confirms rights to the book with a denial of libel or copyright infringement.

ALEXA TRAFFIC RANK: 2,610,280

AUTHOR-FRIENDLY RATING: In the previous version of this book, this company was rated "0." The situation has improved dramatically (my guess is that Foremost Press bought out Action Tales).

Publishing fees are fair and one of the cheapest around. The fees include light editing, which is a bargain. A book cover costs extra, but even with this added expense, the total fee is much lower compared with other POD publishing prices. The only downside is the 120 day notice to terminate requirement, which is longer than most.

The publisher's cover art quality is questionable. The sample cover from the publisher left a lot to be desired. The author, however, is not required to use the publisher's cover designer.

Aside from favorable publishing fees, Foremost Press offers these positives:

1. Author purchases copies for 50% of the retail price, which is better than most other publishers (except for BookPros and Dog Ear Publishing).
2. Foremost Press may be the only POD publisher which doesn't charge the author the annual fee charged by Lightning Source, the printer used by most PODs.
3. Foremost Press offers book registration on Booksense (www.booksense.com). It instructs the author to register on his own or to pay $47 to Foremost Press to do it for you.

Foremost Press is honest and upfront. It tops the list and is almost within reach of the Outstanding Publisher category.

GOLDEN PILLAR PUBLISHING
www.goldenpillarpublishing.com

FORMAT OF BOOKS: paperback and hardcover

GENRES ACCEPTED: All

PUBLISHING FEES: There are three publishing packages:

Bronze Package $500 (www.goldenpillarpublishing.com/bronze.html) includes:

- Basic cover design
- ISBN
- 12 free copies of the book
- Listing in Bowker's Books In Print
- Listing book with Amazon.com and BarnesandNoble.com
- One-page press release announcing the publication
- Provides a completed copyright registration form

Silver Package $1,500 (www.goldenpillarpublishing.com/silver.html) includes everything in the Bronze Package, plus:

- Illustrated cover in full-color
- Red-line edit of the manuscript
- Copy of the book archived on CD-Rom
- 24 free copies of the book
- Listing with Borders.com
- Full-color press release
- Copyright registration

Gold Package $3,500 (www.goldenpillarpublishing.com/gold.html) includes everything in the Bronze and Silver packages plus:

- Premium, full-color cover with originally commissioned cover illustration (author can request changes up to three times during the design phase)
- 48 copies of the book

ROYALTIES PAID TO AUTHOR:

70% of the Gross Profit for the Bronze Package

80% of the Gross Profit for the Silver Package

90% of the Gross Profit for the Gold Package

The Gross Profit is the wholesale price less the production costs. The wholesale price is 55% of the suggested retail price of the book. For example:

A 5"x 8" paperback costs $.90 + $.013 x number of pages.

A 280-page paperback costs $4.54 or ($.90 + $.013 x 280 pages). This publisher sets the suggested retail price at $19.95 and 55% of that is $8.98 (the wholesale price). Thus, the gross profit is $8.98 – $4.54 or $4.44.

The royalty for one book sale in the Bronze Package is $3.01. The royalty for one book sale in the Silver Package is $3.55. The royalty for one book sale in the Gold Program is $3.99.

NOTABLE PROVISIONS OF THE PUBLISHING AGREEMENT: The contract is available at http://www.golden-pillarpublishing.com/agreement.pdf.

Paragraph 1, "License of Rights," gives the publisher world-wide exclusive rights for hardcover or paperback (depending on which box the author checks) until terminated by either party. The contract can terminate several ways, including upon the publisher's bankruptcy and/or its cessation of business operations by the publisher. Either party can also terminate the agreement at any time by giving 30 days written notice.

Paragraph 5.1 specifies that the royalties are a percentage of the Net Revenues, which is the same as the publisher's web site description of "gross profits."

Paragraph 11 allows the publisher's legal counsel to review the author's manuscript to ensure that it doesn't violate copyright laws, contain defamatory material, or otherwise violate applicable laws. If the publisher requests changes based on the publisher's legal counsel's recommendations and the author refuses, then the publisher has "the right to terminate this Agreement without further obligation." The language, "without further obligation," may mean that if the author doesn't make the requested changes, the publisher is not required to refund the publishing fee. In this event, the author should make sure that all publishing fees are refunded and the necessary language requiring the refund is included in the contract.

Don't let Paragraph 18 scare you. The author appoints the publisher as its attorney-in-fact so that the publisher can register the author's copyright and carry out other such administrative matters. The power of attorney is limited to such administrative purposes and does not give the publisher the power to do whatever it wants with the book.

The Author's warranties and indemnification are standard and reasonable.

Paragraph 32 upholds the final written contract as binding. It's important to make sure all publisher obligations are written into the contract.

Paragraphs 40 and 41 call for mediation or arbitration of disputes in Sacramento, California. The author should request modification to the language to allow the author to appear at the mediation or arbitration by telephone. The loser in any legal proceeding pays all the costs and attorneys' fees of the winning party.

ALEXA TRAFFIC RANK: No data

AUTHOR-FRIENDLY RATING: The contract requires only 30 days written notice, and the author retains 100% control of the rights. Of all the POD/epublisher contracts I've reviewed, this is one of the few that was drafted by an attorney. It is thorough and complete. Make sure the contract covers every obligation the publisher promised, whether oral or written via e-mail, or otherwise. According to Section 32, any agreement not written into the contract carries no weight.

The publishing fees are high, but not out of line. By the time you add in the 12 free copies, the press release, and the completed copyright application, the Bronze Package becomes a decent value (the cost of those three items alone is worth $150–$300).

The best deal may be the Silver Package. This package includes a red-line edit (meaning that the edited text is highlighted to distinguish it from unedited portions of a document) of your book. A good line edit is worth $800 to $1000. You also get 24 free copies, which is handy for marketing and promotions as well and for sending copies to book reviewers. The publisher also submits copyright registration, which is worth between $85 and $100.

Royalty percentages are excellent, but the retail price set by the publisher is too high. A $19.95, 280-page paperback by a fledgling writer will have trouble selling. The production costs for the book is $4.54. If the publisher sets the retail price at $15.00 instead of $19.95, and Amazon.com takes its 55% trade discount, there still remains approximately $2.46 to split between the publisher and author. The author makes less per book at this retail price, but more from increased sales. The key to success for a first-time or fledgling writer is sales. If you can post decent sales figures, you'll have more success convincing traditional publishers and agents to consider your subsequent books.

The retail price of books is just too high.

THIRD MILLENNIUM PUBLISHING
www.3mpub.com

FORMAT OF BOOKS: ebooks and POD

GENRES ACCEPTED: All

PUBLISHING FEES: $300 which includes:
- Manuscript preparation for publication
- Summary, description, and biography pages for inclusion on the publisher's web site
- Set up of services which collect money from purchasers
- Cover with commercial clipart and graphic software (although author can provide own)
- Two years display and sales of book on publisher's web site (after two years, $100 per year)

ROYALTIES PAID TO AUTHOR: Royalty equals the selling price of the book less the cost of credit card processing ($.50 plus 2.6% of the selling price) per transaction and less $1 per book publisher's fee.

For example, for a $10 selling price on an ebook, the author receives $8.14 ($10 – (.50 + .26) – $1). For paperback sales, the fee is built into the wholesale price.

In order to lower costs and increase royalties for print books, the author must invest in inventory. For books over 126 pages, the author pays a flat fee for copies regardless of page count. The price ranges from $7.50 to $11 depending on the order size. If an author retails a book for $15, he would need to keep some inventory with the publisher to make any real money. Let's say the author purchases 100 books which he retails at $15, but stores them at the publisher's location. The author's royalty is $6.61 ($15 – $7.50 (cost of book) – $.89 (credit card processing fees)). You can't get many better deals in POD publishing.

PRICE OF BOOKS: Author determines the price, although the publisher suggests setting the ebook price between $4 and $6 and paperback price between $15 and $20.

NOTABLE PROVISIONS OF THE PUBLISHING AGREEMENT: "Third Millennium Publishing Electronic Work Hosting Agreement" is available upon request from the publisher. Many of the important terms are covered at http://3mpub.com/services.

Section B(5) is perhaps the most important term. Any format which the publisher creates for the book is the publisher's property. After termination of the agreement, the publisher has no obligation to provide the formatted file of the book. When asked about this clause, the publisher responded as follows:

> "The author owns the book and the right to publish the book, but we own the files that we created

to produce the book . . . . If the author's book becomes a best seller, we will aid that author in transferring to a high volume printer when the volume exceeds our printing capacity. In such cases, we provide the necessary files reformatted for the printer. We have done so 3–4 times now, both for authors who wanted to buy a lot of commercially printed books to obtain the lower unit price, and for authors who have used other services, such as Booksurge, in addition to Third Millennium Publishing. We also provide files to authors who request them for archival purposes. However, to prevent misunderstandings, we include Section B(5) in our agreement."

It's clear from this response that the author maintains control of all rights to the book and can still sell it anywhere while it's being sold on the publisher's web site. Also, the author can remove the book from the web site at any time. Go to www.3mpub.com/services/faqs.htm which provides a FAQs section. The publisher states, "We do not own the rights to publish your book . . . you own those rights . . . ."

The FAQs section also states that the publisher advertises in both *Writer's Digest* and *Writer's Journal* and registers the author's name and book in the top 100 search engines.

ALEXA TRAFFIC RANK: 1,305,090

AUTHOR-FRIENDLY RATING: The $300 fee is low, but the only way for the author to make the service worthwhile is to purchase 50 to 100 books up front because the larger volume decreases per book costs, which in turn allows the author to set a competitive book price. This of course, increases the basic cost of the package, but such an increase is worth it.

Third Millennium Publishing doesn't offer bells and whistles, but it runs a solid operation. After all, the owner, Michael McCollum, is an author who has sold 250,000 copies of his own books through Ballantine/Del Ray over a 10-year period.

The only reason this publisher isn't in the Outstanding category is because it doesn't give authors the computer files containing book covers, layout, etc. upon termination.

WRITERS WORLD

www.writersworld.co.uk

FORMAT OF BOOKS: paperback POD only

GENRES ACCEPTED: All

PUBLISHING FEES:

Standard Package £1,598 ($2,753 USD) which includes:

- Preparation of the book for POD within 90 days
- ISBN
- Loading and submission the to numerous worldwide databases to increase availability via the Internet and thousands of retail outlets
- Promotion on the worldwide Ingram Advantage Programme
- Distribution of copies to the Legal Deposit Libraries (UK version of the US Copyright Office)
- Submission to Amazon's "Read Inside a Book" programme
- Submission to Google's "Read Inside a Book Programme" (a person doing a subject matter Google search may pick up your name, book title, or content)
- Listing on www.bookinformation.co.uk , which is part of

The Book Trust

This package does not include design, layout, formatting, consulting, editing, or proof-reading services.

The author supplies cover art and pays an additional £48 for deposit of the book to the legal deposit libraries that maintain the national archives of the British Isles (required).

Enhanced Service £1,998, ($3,486.12) which includes:

- Standard package services
- Professional editing for spelling, punctuation, and grammar
- Four-color cover

Both plans make the author's book available through major Internet bookshops, including Amazon.com, BarnesandNoble.com, Waterstones, WHSmith, Ottakar's, Hammicks, Blackwells, Thins, Methvens, and more, and other web sites throughout Europe, the Far East, Australia, and the U.S.

ROYALTIES PAID TO AUTHOR: 100% of sales price less the printing cost ($.015 per page and $.90 per cover) and less the trade discount, if applicable.

NOTABLE PROVISIONS OF THE PUBLISHING AGREEMENT: The contract is available at www.writersworld.co.uk/contract.asp.

This one-page agreement covers little. Section 2, "Intellectual Property Rights," states the obvious: the writer lacks the right to use the publisher's name, and the publisher acknowledges that the writer holds all rights to the work.

Section 4 places venue for all legal disputes in UK courts, which is inconvenient for American residents.

Anyone considering signing the publisher's contract should first clarify these issues in writing: (1) the contract's term or duration, (2) the rights and procedure to terminate the contract, and

(3) the author's right to receive the edited version of work if the author terminates the contract.

ALEXA TRAFFIC RANK: 979,378

AUTHOR-FRIENDLY RATING: Pretty Good. The publishing fees are excessive, but the charge for copies offsets the up-front publishing fees.

The publishing agreement is not comprehensive. Its vagueness leaves too many unresolved and unaddressed issues which will quite likely give rise to disagreement between the author and publisher.

If the author doesn't reside in the UK, there's no reason to consider signing with Writers World, unless the book is targeted to the international community and would benefit from listings on well-known, online bookstores in other countries.

This publisher has potential, assuming there is no term and you can cancel at any time (which appears as though you can).

CHAPTER 8

Publishers Who Are Just Okay

If none of the Outstanding or Pretty Good publishers discussed in this book fits your needs or will publish your work, then by all means comb the Just Okay group to see if a publisher meets your requirements.

What does "Just Okay" mean? It means just what you think it means—that it's something less than average, but not horrible. The editor of this book suggested I call this category "Middle of the Road", but frankly, the publishers here are not quite "middle of the road."

There are many publishers far better than ones covered in this chapter. These Just Okay publishers offer deficient and over-priced products and services, and have problem issues which preclude them from inclusion in the other ratings.

However, these publishers (such as Trafford and Xlibris) probably aren't scams or fly-by-nights which is why they're on my Just Okay list instead of my Publishers-To-Avoid list.

I suggest only considering a publisher in the Just Okay category, if you can't get a publisher in either the Outstanding or Pretty Good groups to accept your work.

AUTHORS ONLINE
www.authorsonline.co.uk

FORMAT OF BOOKS: paperback and ebooks

GENRES ACCEPTED: All

PUBLISHING FEES: This is a UK company and all fees are in British pounds.

£95 ($165 USD) Electronic publishing in various formats: Adobe Acrobat and Microsoft Reader

£550 ($960 USD) POD Standard Service (European Union residents only)

£468 ($817 USD) POD Standard Service (non-European Union residents)

POD Standard Services includes these services:

- Publication in paperback
- Publication in ebook
- Five review copies that can be ordered at cost. Additional copies can be ordered at cost plus 25% of the retail price for resale.
- Supplied to the UK's leading book distributors (Gardners or Bertrams)
- Supplied to Ingram's in the U.S. and Canada
- Make book available for sale on Amazon (Amazon.com if published in the U.S. or Amazon.co.uk if published in the UK)
- Cover for additional fee £60–£250(4104–$236 USD) Otherwise, author supplies cover.

The publisher doesn't make it clear whether it receives a trade discount for sales on its own web site. Author should seek clarification. If the publisher takes a discount, this would be double-dipping.

NOTABLE PROVISIONS OF THE PUBLISHING AGREEMENT: "Rights and Duties of The Company," Paragraph 3, describes the royalty payment structure.

"Rights and Duties of the Author or Agent or Publisher," Paragraph 2, gives the publisher the exclusive right to publish an electronic version of the book during the term of the contract and the exclusive right to sell the print version within "the territorial boundaries of the United Kingdom and any other territory the author may specify." Author gives the publisher the exclusive right of publication in the UK only; no reference is made to the U.S. or any other country.

"Rights and Duties of the Author or Agent or Publisher," Paragraphs 17 and 18, seem contradictory. Paragraph 17 says that the parties will attempt to resolve any disputes via alternate dispute resolution prior to commencing legal action. Paragraph 18 states that the parties will be bound by any decision given by the Alternative Dispute Resolution process, thus taking away the right to commence court action.

ALEXA TRAFFIC RANK: 1,103,048

AUTHOR-FRIENDLY RATING: The package prices are high, even for UK standards, and the fees are also extremely high, especially when you convert them into U.S. dollars. The standard package doesn't include a cover. Neither package includes ISBN or bar code service, which translates to more expenses for the author. Refer to http://www.authorsonline.co.uk/eBooks/AonL%20Publishing%20Details.pdf. It is cheaper to purchase the Standard POD package and pay for the editing/proofreading/review service and book cover design à la carte, than to purchase the Enhanced Package.

The contract is also confusing and contains omissions, such

as the term of the contract. It took several requests sent via e-mail to gain clarification. Here's a portion of my e-mail request and the publishing company's response:

ML: "Basically, the way I read your contract the author can terminate at any time and your exclusive to publish is only good as long as the author chooses to keep his book with you."

Company: "That is correct—it was because of the old printing contract we had with our distributors but now the arrangement has changed and the author can terminate at any time they want. Very few ever have, I hasten to add!"

So, there you have it. If you sign with this company, make sure the publisher includes similar language in the contract.

I appreciated the company's prompt and open response. That's a real positive in my book: people with nothing to hide.

Although I think the company is honest, UK authors can find a better deal elsewhere. U.S.-based writers have no reason to consider this publisher, mostly because of its distribution practices and high pricing.

FUSION PRESS

http://www.authorlink.com/fusion/fp_welcome.htm

FORMAT OF BOOKS: paperback

GENRES ACCEPTED: At the publisher's discretion: "We do not provide indiscriminate subsidy publishing for individual authors. To qualify for our publishing services you must be an established publisher or an established author/organization/entity with a tax ID number."

PUBLISHING FEES: There are two publishing packages fully described at www.authorlink.com/fusion/fp_fees.htm.

Basic Book Publishing $795 includes:

- Standard full color cover (from templates)
- One hard copy galley proof
- One set of galley proof corrections
- Web page on Authorlink.com for six months
- Order processing and fulfillment

Complete Book Publishing $1,195 includes all the Basic Book Publishing plan features, plus:

- customized full-color cover
- US Copyright registration
- ISBN
- Inclusion in Books In Print
- UPC bar code
- Registration with Amazon.com, BarnesandNoble.com, and Borders.com

ROYALTIES PAID TO AUTHOR: 40% of the net income per sale, which is about 8% to 15% of the retail price. According to the publisher, book production costs are $8.97 per book, leaving $3.57 in net income (based on a typical 300-page book that sells for $14.95). Thus, the author makes $1.42, or 9% of the retail price.

NOTABLE PROVISIONS OF THE PUBLISHING AGREEMENT: The publishing agreement is unavailable.

ALEXA TRAFFIC RANK: 470,979

AUTHOR-FRIENDLY RATING: Fusion Press is a highly reputable company, and the fees are not out of line. The killer here is the royalties. They are simply too low for this type of publishing.

Its Rights Showcase Listing and New Media Listing services can provide excellent exposure for authors seeking agents and traditional publishers. You can learn about these services at http://

authorlink.com/asublist_gold.html (Rights Showcase Listing) and www.authorlink.com/selflist.html (New Media Listing). The company claims that 45% to 65% of the manuscripts listed here are requested by agents or publishers and that authors of 20% to 25% of these requested manuscripts are later offered representation.

However, the production costs are among the highest I've seen in POD publishing. Author copies cost almost $10 ($8.97 plus $.99 shipping cost per book). This cost is acceptable only if the quality of its books matches the quality of Random House paperbacks. Also, the author must order copies in quantities of 25 or more.

The Basic Book Publishing Plan doesn't include a custom cover or ISBN. For its price, these services should offer these features. The Complete Book Publishing Plan is a better deal, although still a bit high. The package would be much more valuable if it included listings in the Rights Showcase or the New Media.

Another disadvantage is that the publisher refuses to accept phone calls.

Fusion Press's web site does not mention exclusive rights or contain terms that aren't author-friendly. A request and follow-up inquiry for a copy of the contract went unanswered.

If you want to enjoy the benefits of being affiliated with Authorlink through Fusion Press, list your book on the Rights Showcase or New Media sections of the web site for less than $100 and publish your book with a less expensive POD publisher.

INDY PUBLISH
www.indypublish.com

FORMAT OF BOOKS: ebooks and POD (paperback and hardback)

GENRES ACCEPTED: All

PUBLISHING FEES: There are five publishing packages described at: www.indypublish.com/PublishingServices/sv_sc_index.asp.

Basic is free and includes:

- Standard cover design
- Up to five corrections by author
- Available as a paperback and ebook
- ISBN
- UPC/EAN bar code
- Registration with Books-In-Print
- Sales through Amazon.com, BarnesandNoble.com, Borders.com, and the publisher's online store
- Publisher designs a web site for the book with a unique URL

Bronze $189 includes features in the Basic package plus:

- Custom-designed four color book cover
- Author's option to submit picture or graphic for the cover
- Up to 25 corrections by author after submission
- 100 bookmarks, 100 postcards, and 100 business cards featuring book
- Free copy of the POD version of the book

Silver $285 includes everything in the Bronze package plus:

- Customized interior book design
- Author's option to submit 10 graphics for the interior design
- LOON number

Gold $575 includes everything in the Silver package plus:

- Author option to submit 20 graphics for the interior design
- Author option to include an index and up to five tables in the book interior

- Up to 50 corrections by author after submission
- Book availability as a hard cover
- Copyright registration

Platinum $999 includes everything in the Gold plus:

- Author option to submit five pictures or graphics for cover design and up to 30 graphics for the interior design
- Author option to include an index and up to 10 tables and footnotes in the book interior
- Up to 100 corrections by author after submission

Authors purchase copies at a 25% discount off the retail price for orders up to 19 copies of their book; a 30% discount for orders of 20–99; and a 35% discount for orders over 100.

ROYALTIES PAID TO THE AUTHOR: The complete book pricing and royalty calculator is at http://www.indypublish. com/PublishingServices/Sv_P&R_calculate.php.

Ebooks royalty is 50% of the amount received by the publisher less a $.50 transaction fee per book. This calculation nets the author about $.75 per sale.

Print books royalty is 50% of the sales price less printing costs and any discounts received or fees paid to third party vendors. The author's royalty is about 13% of the selling price for books sold by third party vendors, such as Amazon.com, and about 29% of retail price for books sold through the publisher's online store.

The author may set the price of the book so long as the price exceeds a publisher- specified minimum.

NOTABLE PROVISIONS OF THE PUBLISHING AGREEMENT: Section 5 "Rights" makes it clear that the author only grants non-exclusive rights for both print and electronic books during the term of the agreement, which lasts until one party gives 30 days written notice. The last sentence clarifies that the author retains all subsidiary rights.

Section 6 "Author Warranties" and Section 7 "Indemnities" are standard and reasonable.

Section 9 "Terms" clarifies that the "Author may enter into other publishing agreements for the same work." Authors who choose the Basic Package should direct their attention to the second paragraph. If the publisher lists the book for sale on its web site and fewer than 12 copies are sold in the first year, the author must pay $50 to keep the book listing on the web site.

Section 10 "Book Price Determination" allows the author to set the book's retail price so long as it exceeds the publisher's minimum price (http://www.indypublish.com/PublishingServices/Sv_P&R_calculate.php).

Section 12 provides that Virginia law is the operating law for contract interpretation, and any legal disputes will be heard in Virginia.

Section 13 "Notices" describes the procedure to give notice and terminate the contract.

ALEXA TRAFFIC RANK: 2,001,491

AUTHOR-FRIENDLY RATING: The contract is author-friendly and easy to terminate. The Basic package is free and gives the author almost everything but the cover. After the Basic package, the Bronze Package is the best deal unless you require graphics, indexes, tables, and other similar features.

Two downsides of Indy Publish:

1. The minimum retail price of print books. If the minimum retail price is $8.84 for a 125-page book, what's will be the price for a 250- to 300-page book? A high-price book by a little-known author is risky.
2. The charge to the author for copies, which is 25% of the retail price. A 230-page paperback on an order of 19 or fewer books costs $8.48 each. This price is acceptable, but

if the author chooses to have a higher retail price for his book, the cost for author copies becomes prohibitive. For example, if an author chooses to retail a 230-page paperback for $15, she pays $11.25 per copy. So, an author is punished if she wants to earn more in royalties because the tradeoff is paying more for her copies of her own book (even though the cost to print the books remains the same). This is reason enough to skip this publisher.

LLUMINA PRESS

www.llumina.com

FORMAT OF BOOKS: POD and ebooks

GENRES ACCEPTED: All (accepts between 70%-80% of all submissions)

PUBLISHING FEES: There are three publishing packages: $699 for paperback; $759 for hardcover; and $899 for paperback and hardcover. If you want to sell your book as an ebook, add another $65 to any package.

All packages (www.llumina.com/prices.htm) include:
- ISBN numbers for print and/or hardcover editions
- LCCN
- Submission to Bowker's Books In Print, Amazon.com, BarnesandNoble.com, and other third party retailers
- Typesetting
- Bar code
- Color cover design
- Listing in Ingram and Baker & Taylor
- A web page on the publisher's web site

ROYALTIES PAID TO AUTHOR: Print royalties are 30% of the list price for copies sold through the publisher, and 10% of the list price for copies sold through third party retailers.

Ebook royalties are 60% of the list price for copies sold through the publisher, and 40% of the list price for copies sold through third party retailers.

A complete description of the royalty structure can be found in "Print Royalties" and "Electronic Royalties" of the Author Agreement at www.llumina.com/agree.htm.

NOTABLE PROVISIONS OF THE AUTHOR AGREEMENT: The complete author agreement is at www.llumina.com/agree.htm.

"Term of License" calls for a three-year term, which starts from the date the book is first released for publication, not the date you sign the contract. The author only grants non-exclusive print and electronic rights (see the "License to Publish" section) and can terminate at any time with 30 days written notice (see the "Author Cancellation" section).

At first glance, "Author Cancellation" is troublesome. Its language appears to charge the author, upon the author's contract termination, a cancellation fee in addition to fees paid-to-date. However, when contacted and questioned, the publisher responded:

> "...The $40 an hour fee is for administrative, formatting and design services that may have taken place prior to your notification to cancel. If our publisher, Deborah Greenspan, works on the project herself, her time is billable at $100 an hour. We reserve the right to deduct a reasonable fee for services already rendered if you cancel the contract prior to the publication of the book. Once the book has been published and this fee settled, you can cancel anytime with 30 days written notice, and no further costs would be due. However if you cancel once the book has gone to pub-

lication, no publication costs would be refunded
to you because the book would be finished."

That's fair and reasonable.

"Subsidiary Rights" confirms the author's rights to all film,
television, and other rights.

"Author's Copies" gives the author a 30% discount on an order less than 25; 50% discount for an order of 25 to 99copies;
55% discount for an order of 100 to 299; and 60% discount for
an order of 300 or more copies.

"Publisher Termination" gives the publisher the right to terminate the agreement at any time without refunding the author's
publishing fees if the book has been printed.

"Author Warranties" and "Indemnification" are standard and
reasonable.

"General Provisions" contains no language that requires lawsuits and arbitration proceedings to be physically held in Florida.
The language, "this Agreement is governed by the laws of the State
of Florida," only requires a court or arbitrator to refer to Florida
case law and statutes when interpreting the contract and its terms
and to resolve other similar issues.

ADDITIONAL SERVICES: The cost of marketing and promotional packages range from $429 to $899. All packages include
varying numbers of copies, two press releases, a sell sheet, listing
in Llumina's e-zine, and e-mail of the press release to thousands
of media reviewers. To review these marketing programs, go to
www.llumina.com/marketing.htm. None of the marketing packages does much for me because you could purchase these services
individually and probably pay less.

The $100 price for listing in *Ingram Advance Magazine*, a
monthly catalog mailed to booksellers and libraries worldwide, is
worthwhile. Titles are only eligible to appear once—when they're
first released. Ingram produces a short paragraph about your book
along with pricing information and a black-and-white cover image. You may try to deal directly with Ingram and see if you can be

included in the *Ingram Advance*. It'll likely cost you less than $100, since at least one other publisher, PageFree Publishing, charges only $75.

The Bookstore Return program (www.llumina.com/bookstore_returns.htm) solves one of the bigger problems POD authors face: persuading bookstores to accept non-returnable books. It costs $500 for the first year and $140 each year thereafter to be listed in the catalog that Llumina sends to 2,500 book retailers. To avoid getting lost in the crowd, you'll want to buy advertising space. A quarter-page ad costs $349; a half-page ad costs $549; and a full-page ad costs $1,199.

ALEXA TRAFFIC RANK: 327,079

AUTHOR-FRIENDLY RATING: I sent three e-mails to the publisher for information and received no response. That should tell you something. The only changes in the past year are price increases: add $200 to each package and $65 to ebook publishing. The level of service hasn't changed. Of all the publishers reviewed in this book, Llumina produces the least impressive covers, some bordering on amateurish. Although the up-front fee includes cover art, you may be disappointed with the product.

The retail prices of books are outrageous. Generally, a 250- to 300-page paperback needs to retail for no more than $15 or $16 to remain competitive. One book, *Stay Dead!*, a 272-page paperback retails at $17.95 plus $5.50 in shipping charges! A 312-page, nonfiction paperback, *America's Trading Partners*, retails at $24.95, plus $6.00 in shipping charges.

The retail price of the book directly affects what the author pays for copies. For orders up to 25 copies with a retail price of $17.95, the author pays $12.57 per book. Don't forget shipping charges. How will the author ever sell the book for $15?

Despite the unfavorable prices, the publisher's contract is author-friendly and easy to get out of. The contract provides for fair royalties that border on generous, but these pluses are lost in the sea of poor cover art and over-priced books.

MY EBOOKS
www.mye-books.com

FORMAT: ebooks, paperback, and hardcover

GENRES ACCEPTED: Fiction and nonfiction in all categories, short story collections, and children's books. No erotica. The submission guidelines are available at www.aproposbooks.mye-books.com/submissionguidelinespublishing.htm.

PUBLISHING FEES:

Ebooks $0, if author wants to sell book on the publisher's web site.

Ebooks $60, listing with third party retailers. A cover is provided at no additional cost to the author.

Print Books $375 for paperback and $475 for hardcover. Both fees include cover art.

Editorial services are available for additional charge.

ROYALTIES PAID TO AUTHOR: 30% of the sales price

NOTABLE PROVISIONS OF THE PUBLISHING CONTRACT: The publishing contract is available at www.mye-books.com/publishingcontract.htm.

Section II "Grantor of Rights" gives exclusive print and epublishing rights to the publisher for the term of the agreement.

Section III defines the term of the agreement as two years, starting from the date the book is first available for sale. Either party can terminate with 90 days written notice. However, it's unclear whether the author can cancel by giving 90 days written notice at any time during the term or only after the initial two-year term. Keep in mind that ambiguous language in a contract is generally interpreted by courts in the light most favorable to the party who didn't draft the contract, which is almost always the author.

The publisher's response to my inquiry about this ambiguity is as follows:

> "Basically, it's both. I will keep your book available on the web site for two years unless you give me 90 days notice that you wish to void the contract. My goal is to assist writers. I'm very flexible."

Section VI "Marketing and Promotion" requires publisher to send out at least three review copies.

Section V deals with royalties. The contract discusses "retail download price," which applies to ebooks, but fails to mention retail print price. A review of the publisher's web site shows that the contract is outdated. The author should clarify print royalties with the publisher before signing the contract. It's obvious that this publisher uses an outdated contract which doesn't reflect its additional print publication operations.

The contract doesn't address charges to the author for editing services. However, the publisher's web site states, "If we find numerous errors (more than ten) including, but not limited to, spelling, punctuation and typos, we will charge an editorial fee of $100 to prepare your manuscript for publication" (see http://www.mye-books.com/editorialservices.htm). This is a huge problem for the publisher, since it has no legal right to charge the author for editing, because Section VII "Entire Agreement" clearly states that only what is in the contract rules.

ALEXA TRAFFIC RANK: 4,663,155

AUTHOR-FRIENDLY RATING: Because the author can get out of the contract at any time, the two-year term isn't a big problem. Some other terms are so poorly written that their ambiguity favors the author. Nevertheless, entering into a contract that allows the author to wiggle out with the help of a good lawyer is not reason enough to sign with a publisher. It does appear that the publisher is willing to work with you, so don't write this publisher off completely.

NEW CONCEPTS PUBLISHING (NCP)

www.newconceptspublishing.com

FORMAT OF BOOKS: ebooks and paperback (one-year after release of the ebook)

GENRES ACCEPTED: All genres, although publisher's specialty is romance and its subgenres. Go to www.newconceptspublishing.com/submissionguidelines.htm for a list of editors and the specific genres they currently accept.

PUBLISHING FEES: $0. NCP provides ISBN, cover art, editing, and some promotion of your book.

ROYALTIES PAID TO AUTHOR: 30%-40% of the book's download price (For details, see "What are your royalty rates?" at www.newconceptspublishing.com/faqs.htm).

NOTABLE PROVISIONS OF THE PUBLISHING AGREEMENT: There is no contract available on NCP's web site.

An e-mail request for a contract elicited the following response from senior editor Andrea DePasture: "I'm sorry, but we don't send out a sample contract to nameless people and addresses."

Despite DePasture's response, the web site FAQs provide some information. The publisher takes exclusive rights for two years for short stories and four years for novels and novellas. Also refer to "What is your contract length time?" at www.newconceptspublishing.com/faqs.htm for detailed information. According to the web site FAQs, the author may be able to terminate the contract if a traditional print publisher offers the author a contract:

> FAQ: "If I sell to a paper publisher and they want all rights, can I withdraw my book?"
> ANSWER: "If we have invested time and money in the book, NO. If we have not, then YES."

My gut tells me that NCP's decision to release electronic rights without a fight or demand for compensation will depend on the size and reputation of the paper publisher who offers the author a print contract and less on what this publisher believes it can earn from the sales of the author's book.

There are a few positives about NCP, at least according to the web site FAQs section:

> "We have many ways that we promote NCP and our authors. We participate in literary signings, bookfairs, conferences, trade shows, magazine and newspaper interviews, banner advertising, press releases, contests, sales, trade advertising, etc. Currently, we are focusing on the retail market and are expanding our books into online book-stores as well as physical bookstores. We regularly contact the headquarters of the major chains with proposals and have a contract with Baker & Taylor distributors . . . ."

ALEXA TRAFFIC RANK: 327,718

AUTHOR-FRIENDLY RATING: The only factor keeping NCP in the Just Okay category is that it has been around for 10 years. Its refusal to produce a sample contract and its unwillingness to answer questions about its services pushes it close to the Publishers-to-Avoid category.

Like a traditional publisher, NCP doesn't charge a fee, but it edits your work, creates cover art, and more. But unlike a traditional publisher, it doesn't automatically publish the print book. There is nothing wrong with first testing the book in electronic form. The author must understand that signing a contract with NCP means losing control over the book for the term of the contract which may be as long as four years. The publisher decides when and if the book is published in print.

Three e-mail requests for a copy of the contract and information about the services provided to authors were delivered in September and October 2005. Below is a copy of my last e-mail sent on October 30, 2005:

> "Andrea, I'm writing a book entitled *The Fine Print of Self-Publishing*, which analyzes the contracts and services of the top print-on-demand and eb-ook publishers (www.book-publishers-compared. com). I'm finalizing the 2006 edition and am having a problem reviewing your company because I can't get a copy of your publishing contract.
>
> When I wrote you a few years ago to get a contract, I received this response from you: 'I'm sorry, but we don't send out a sample contract to nameless people and addresses.'
>
> My assistant sent you an e-mail in August and in September requesting information so that I could accurately and fairly review your company. We haven't had any response.
>
> I understand if you don't want to provide this information and will respect your decision to not cooperate. I just want to give you every chance to provide me the information I need to make my review as complete as possible."

Despite the hand-in-my-face attitude this publisher blatantly showed, it's a tough one to call. The upside is that this publisher has been around since 1996, the dawn of epublishing, and performs many of the functions of a traditional publisher, such as editing, creating cover art, and promotion of the book.

For authors of steamier types of romance fiction, NCP may make sense because of its apparent marketing expertise and specialty in this genre. The downside is that the exclusive term may be too long and difficult to set aside.

The web site doesn't state the book's retail price, so it's impossible to judge whether the royalty is fair. It appears that the average download price is $4 to $6. With this limited information, it appears the royalty amount isn't bad.

The long contract term and the publisher's refusal to allow the author to terminate the contract makes NCP a publisher to avoid, but for the fact that it's been around for 10 years.

An author who's considering this publisher should first contact authors who have used NCP's services to ask them about their experiences. Ask these authors whether the publisher's marketing and promotion assistance is as good as it sounds. Make sure you know, understand, and are satisfied with:

- The contract length
- The publisher's rights granted by the author
- The exclusivity or non-exclusivity of the contract
- The requirements to terminate the publishing contract during the term and any ramifications of early termination, such as the publisher's non-exclusive right to continue book sales after termination

At least one writer has filed a complaint with the Georgia Attorney General over nonpayment of royalties. The National Writers Union issued a warning about NCP in 2004 (http://www.nwu.org/PDF/WriterAlert_NCP.pdf).

PLANE TREE PUBLISHING
www.planetree-publishing.com

FORMAT OF BOOKS: POD paperback

GENRES ACCEPTED: All (Manuscripts must be 90,000 words or less, or additional fees apply)

PUBLISHING FEES: £350 GBP ($610 USD) (www.plan-etree-publishing.com/comp.cfm) includes:

- Personalized cover chosen from 20 templates with the author's name, book title, graphics supplied by the author, and blurb about the author on the back
- ISBN, bar code, and registration with Books In Print
- Five books issued to the UK Copyright Libraries

There is an additional charge of £1 for every 300 words after the first 90,000.

The per copy charge for each book printed is £.015 per black & white printed page and £.65 per cover (£4.10 for a 230-page book).

ROYALTIES PAID TO AUTHOR: Section 8 of the publisher's contract states that the author receives 10% of the selling price as a royalty. The Publishing Services page of the web site (www.planetree-publishing.com/comp.cfm) states that the author receives "10% of net selling price on books sold from the PlaneTree web site, 10% minus retailer's 33% when the book is sold in a store, and 10% minus wholesaler's 45% for books sold to wholesalers and distributors." The author should seek clarification from the publisher.

NOTABLE PROVISIONS OF THE PUBLISHING AGREEMENT: The agreement can be downloaded at www.plan-etree-publishing.com/agreement.cfm. The contract is simple and straightforward.

The "Grant of Rights" section gives the publisher the non-exclusive right to publish the book. Either party can terminate the contract at any time.

The "The Author" section lists the author's representations, warranties, and indemnification, which are standard and reasonable.

Any disputes which arise are arbitrated in London, England.

ALEXA TRAFFIC RANK: No Data

AUTHOR-FRIENDLY RATING: Much of the contract is author-friendly, but a 10% royalty is absurd for POD. There is no justifiable reason for an author outside the UK to consider Plane Tree Publishing. Even UK authors can find much better POD deals.

The £350 publishing fee is high, but the price for copies is low enough to prevent placing this publisher in the Publishers-To-Avoid category.

PLEASANT WORD

www.pleasantword.com

FORMAT OF BOOKS: POD

GENRES: Only publishes Christian authors whose books do not contain objectionable material, such as unbiblical theology, challenges to the deity of Jesus Christ, offensive language, and indecent scenes.

PUBLISHING FEES: This publisher offers four packages. Complete details and a comparison of the packages are at http://www.pleasantword.com/default.asp?id=7959.

The White Ribbon Package ($699) is for authors who want their POD book published without marketing or distribution services. It includes:

- ISBN
- Bar code
- Copyright registration
- Choice of ten cover templates

- Authors can purchase copies at 50% discount off the retail cover price

The package price is expensive for the limited services received

The Yellow Ribbon Package ($999) includes:

- Every service in the White Ribbon Package (or equivalent upgrade below)
- Listing at Amazon.com and BarnesandNoble.com
- listing with Baker & Taylor (or a comparable company) so that your book is potentially available at 25,000 book-stores and libraries
- 10 free copies
- 100% royalties on the Net Profits of each sale
- 58% discount off the retail price for author copies
- Cover design using a tool that allows author to select fonts, colors, and more. A designer takes author's stock choices and creates a "custom" cover.

The Red Ribbon Package ($1,399) includes:

- Every service in the Yellow Ribbon Package (or equivalent upgrade below)
- 60% discount off the retail price for author copies
- Customized cover
- 15 copies of the book
- Listing on Pleasantwordbooks.com.

The Blue Ribbon Package ($1,799 plus required editing fees) includes:

- Every service in the Red Ribbon Package (or equivalent upgrade below)
- 62% discount off the retail price for author copies
- 30 copies of the book
- E-mail announcement to the publisher's trade list of 1,000 Christian bookstores

- • Promotion at the Christian Booksellers Association convention

The required editing costs at least $2 per page for a simple proofread (all editing and additional fees can be found at http://www.pleasantword.com/default.asp?id=8218#88).

ROYALTIES PAID TO AUTHOR: 100% of the net profit. Net Profit is the retail sale price less the bookseller's discount, the printing cost, and the handling fee of $1.95 per book sold on Pleasantword.com, if any. For details on retail pricing, handling fees, and bookseller discounts, refer to http://www.pleasantword. com/default.asp?id=8288).

Based on the publisher's figures, a cover cost of $.90, and purchase of the Blue Ribbon Package, which is the most expensive publishing package, the wholesale price of a 230-page, 5.5" x 8.5" paperback is $7.80. However, Pleasant Word's real cost to produce a 230-page book using POD technology is $3.89, not $7.80. Most PODs use Lightning Source for printing and pay $.013–$.015 per page plus $.90 per cover. This analysis shows that it's misleading for Pleasant Word to state that the author receives 100% of the net profit since its cost of printing is double the normal price.

The 27% discount is basically yours to play with. If you want to sell the book for less than the actual retail price, you can lower it as much as 27%. This is a great feature. The author can take the 230-page book that retails for $17.99 and sell it for up to $4.86 less.

Only $3.90 of the $17.99 sale price goes to production costs, which leaves $14.09. From $14.09, the publisher takes another $5.85, $3.90 for printing costs, and $1.95 for the handling fee. If the author sells the book without any other discounts, the author receives a net royalty of 46%, or $8.24.

SELLING PRICE OF THE BOOKS: Depends on the trim size and whether the book is hardcover or paperback. A 200- to 249-page paperback with a trim size of 5.5" x 8.5" or 6" x 9", retails for $17.99. A full discussion and examples of retail pricing are available at www.pleasantword.com/default.asp?id=8316.

NOTABLE PROVISIONS OF THE PUBLISHING AGREEMENT: The publishing agreement can be found at http://pleasantword.com/default.asp?id=8211.

"Author Right to Ownership" grants to the publisher a non-exclusive right to print and publish the work. The author can sell and distribute the book while the contract is in effect, and can also terminate the contract at any time. While the author owns the book and the cover concept, the publisher owns the text files or layout and the actual file containing the cover and art. In light of the price paid by the author, the author should receive ownership of these files.

"Copyright, ISBN/ Library of Congress" states that the publisher will procure an ISBN, register the copyright in your name, and obtain an LCCN. These add-on services are a nice perk because the services alone are worth between $150 and $175.

"Publisher's Rights" outlines offensive materials that the publisher will not publish, such as books that promote the Word of Faith or Prosperity doctrine, the Brownsville/Toronto "revival," and women pastors in leadership over men. If an author submits other material, such as unbiblical theology, challenges to the deity of Jesus Christ, offensive language, indecent scenes, or suggestive dialogue, the publisher will allow the Author to modify the material, but will charge at least $200 for "fees and costs" incurred "up to the point of determination of objectionable material."

"Term and Termination" allows three years for the publisher's non-exclusive license, although either party may terminate the contract with 30 days written notice.

"Dispute Resolution" requires parties to resolve disputes through arbitration in King County, Washington. If both parties agree, they may mediate instead of arbitrate a dispute.

ADDITIONAL SERVICES: Various marketing and publicity packages are available from $495 to $1,995. For details, go to www.pleasantword.com/default.asp?id=7994 .

ALEXA TRAFFIC RANK: 3,697,394

AUTHOR-FRIENDLY RATING: Just okay. Christian publishing is a wonderful option for many authors. However, Pleasant Word cloaks its services with religion, which may deter authors from questioning its fees. Pleasant Word's web site FAQs defines its mission:

> "We are all brothers and sisters in Jesus Christ. We're not here to promote ourselves, but to glorify God by serving our authors and the church. Of course we offer a thoroughly professional and friendly service but, rather than following the pattern of the world and boasting about ourselves, we know that we are accountable before God for the honesty, integrity, and quality of our work."

I'm not sure if one who doubles the cost to print a book for an author without telling the author is doing much to glorify God. It's more honest to admit doubling the price instead of making authors think that the cost to produce the book is much higher than its actual cost.

The package prices are much too high for services rendered. The author spends $999 for services he can receive from a different publisher for $750. For $999 spent with Pleasant Word, the author only receives a template cover. A Christian author whose book targets the Christian market may want to consider Red Ribbon Package because the package receives appropriate promotion in the Christian venues, but you are still paying way too much. Also, an author may question the publisher's "objectionable material" clause because its language is broad and may allow the publisher to indiscriminately make another $200.

On the other hand, the royalties are fabulous. The author's ability to give readers a discount up to 27% of the retail price is advantageous because the author can tweak the price to determine the optimal price. For books with Christian subject matter, the marketing opportunities such as the Christian Booksellers Association (CBA) convention, make this publisher one to consider.

The contract is reasonable, except for the publisher's right to collect another $200 for material it subjectively deems "objectionable."

The only package worth considering is the Red Ribbon Package. This publisher may offer decent opportunities for Christian authors, but its tactic of referring to God when explaining its business practices doesn't necessarily mean it will give you a great deal.

PUBLISH TO GO
www.publishtogo.com

FORMAT OF BOOKS: ebooks and POD

GENRES ACCEPTED: All. The company operates more as a printing or ebook preparation company than as a publisher.

PUBLISHING FEES: A complete breakdown of the publishing fees is at www.publishtogo.com/prices.htm.

This is an à la carte service that prepares your book for sale as an ebook on Amazon.com. The cost for doing this is $225 and includes ISBN, bar code, and submission to Amazon.com.

If your book is not already formatted as a PDF, prices for this service start at $75 (for up to 100 pages).

POD services are on a quote basis only.

ROYALTIES PAID TO THE AUTHOR: Doesn't pay royalties because it isn't a publisher. The Author keeps all sales monies.

NOTABLE PROVISIONS OF THE PUBLISHING AGREEMENT: The complete contract is in the scroll-down box at www.publishtogo.com/orderform.htm.

"Rights" makes it clear that the author retains all rights and can publish the book in any format elsewhere.

The "Warranties" section is standard and reasonable.

"Relationship of Parties" is standard in most commercial contracts where one party provides services to another. Nothing the author does can bind the publisher, as is true for the reverse.

"Term and Termination" indicates that the contract endures until either party submits written notice, including via e-mail. The termination is effective immediately. The clause also specifies that the publisher registers the ISBN and lists itself, not the author, as the "publisher." This means that if the author publishes the book elsewhere after termination, the author must obtain a new ISBN or pay Publish To Go a royalty to use the original ISBN.

"Limitation of Liability" is formatted in ALL CAPITAL LETTERS, so the author can't deny its existence. It states that the publisher isn't liable for any amount which exceeds the original publishing fee.

"General" permits the publisher to change the contract terms by a posting on its web site; such new terms become effective after 30 days. The onus is on the author to periodically check the web site for relevant updates. An author who disagrees with any contract changes can always terminate the contract before the 30 days expire

ALEXA TRAFFIC RANK: No Data

AUTHOR-FRIENDLY RATING: The publisher charges high fees for ebook publication. The only reason the author needs an ISBN is so that the publisher can list the book on Amazon.com. The web site hasn't been updated in more than a year, and many of its links don't work. Also, the author must already have a cover and layout to use this company.

If you're an experienced self-publisher, you can find these services for less elsewhere. If this is your first ebook, you're better off giving up some royalties and going with a free epublisher that will provide similar services and sometimes more, such as the cover design.

SIRIUS PUBLICATIONS
http://sirius-books.com

FORMAT OF BOOK: ebook and paperback

GENRES ACCEPTED: Fiction (especially romance), non-fiction (especially how-to, writer's reference books and self-help), short stories (5,000–50,000 words, especially sci-fi).

However, the submission page at http://sirius-books.com/ssubmissions.html states that Sirius Publications is only interested in previously published books or unpublished short story collections. It also states that it will open submissions in late 2002 to unpublished book length manuscripts. Either this company has neglected its web site, or it's barely in business.

PUBLISHING FEES:

$0 for ebooks

$199 one-time fee for an exclusive or non-exclusive POD contract

$500 for an exclusive POD and ebook package

$25 per year hosting fee for all PODs books

ROYALTIES TO AUTHOR: Depends on whether the author signs an exclusive or non-exclusive POD and/or ebook contracts (discussed more fully below).

NOTABLE PROVISIONS OF THE PUBLISHING AGREEMENT: There are five different contracts. Author's choice depends on whether the publisher receives exclusive or non-exclusive print rights, ebook rights, or both print and ebook rights. Clauses found in all agreements are discussed at the end of this section.

The Ebook non-exclusive contract is available at www.sirius-books.com/ebnonex-contract2.html:

Paragraph I grants the publisher five-year, non-exclusive, worldwide electronic rights to publish the work in any online format, including CD-Rom, Diskette, and DVD.

Paragraph XIII allows the author to grant non-exclusive rights to other publishers during the term of the contract. The author may also terminate the contract at any time during the term with 10 days written notice.

Royalties are 50% of the "net revenue" from each sale. Net revenue equals the retail price of the book less returns and discounts and fees, including credit card transaction fees. The publisher may hold up to 10% of the royalties owed as a reserve against these expenses.

The Ebook exclusive contract is available at www.sirius-books.com/ebex-contract.html:

Provisions match those found in the Ebook non-exclusive contract discussed above, except that Paragraph I makes the publisher's e-rights exclusive for five years and royalties are 60% of the "net revenue" from each sale. Paragraph XIII allows the author to terminate with 10 days written notice.

Given the author's right to terminate during the term of the agreement, the author might as well sign the exclusive ebook contract and collect the extra 10% in royalties. The author should first confirm that the author can cancel with 10 days written notice. Confirmation in writing is always the safest tactic.

The non-exclusive POD contract is available at http://sirius-books.com/podex-contract.html:

Paragraph I gives the publisher five-year, non-exclusive print rights, which means the author may still give non-exclusive print rights to others.

Paragraph XIII confirms that the author can still terminate the contract with 10 days written notice.

Paragraph II requires the author to pay a $199 fee to set up POD printing and a $25 per year maintenance fee. The author receives 60% of the net revenues generated the first year or until

Author earns $100 in royalties, whichever comes first. "Net Revenue" is defined as the "retail price for the work . . . less returns and discounts and overhead (including but not limited to credit card transaction fees)." After that, royalties are 15% of the net revenue.

Paragraph IV gives the publisher the right to withhold a 10% reserve against returns.

The exclusive POD contract is available at http://sirius-books.com/podex-contract.html:

Paragraph I grants to the publisher five-year exclusive print rights.

Paragraph III gives the author to the right to terminate this contract at any time with 90 days written notice.

Paragraph V states that author royalties are 35% for the entire term of the contract.

The author must pay the $199 set-up fee and $25 per year maintenance fee.

The exclusive ebook and POD contract is available at www.sirius-books.com/epex-contract.html:

Paragraph I grants to the publisher one-year worldwide, exclusive print and electronic rights.

Paragraph XIII allows the author to terminate the agreement with 10 days written notice.

Paragraph IV states that author royalties are 70% of the net revenues from electronic sales and 80% of the net revenues from POD sales for the first year or until royalties total $100. After that, POD royalties are 50% of the net revenue of each sale. The publisher may withhold a 10% reserve against returns.

The author must pay the $199 set- up fee and $25 per year maintenance fee.

Clauses Common to ALL Contracts: All contracts contain Paragraph VI copyright language, which states, "It is understood that all rights to print or publish electronically do hereby remain the exclusive rights of Sirius Publications." This statement contradicts the other language in the contracts. During the term of the exclusive ebook, exclusive POD, or the exclusive combination of the two, this sentence may be true, but is never true for the non-exclusive contracts. The author should point this discrepancy out to the publisher and modify the contract accordingly before signing it. This inconsistency is probably either a misprint ("Sirius Publications" should be "author") or a leftover provision from an older version of the contract.

Paragraph XII has "other sales" clauses which address various sales avenues and the author's royalties in such circumstances.

Each clause is explained below, with the applicable contract(s) in parenthesis:

"Royalties On Books Sold at Conferences, Signings, etc., in stores, either online or physical" (appears in all contracts).

The author allows the publisher to sell the book on Amazon. com and other online or offline retailers. Author's royalty is 25% of the "net retail price" (previously defined) after the store's discount.

For example, if the book's retail price is $15 and Amazon.com takes a 50% discount, the author's royalty will be 25% of the net retail price of $7.50.

There is no reason not to accept this clause, as its terms may only increase sales avenues. However, an author in a non-exclusive contract may want to avoid a situation where both the author and publisher send copies to the same seller, such as Amazon.com, at different prices. The author's decision whether to accept this clause depends on how aggressive he plans to be in selling the same version of the book that the publisher is selling under a non-exclusive contract.

"Author Initiated Sales" doesn't require the author to initial or agree to anything. If you initiate a bulk order for any version other than the one for which the publisher has an exclusive, there would be no reason to share your good fortune with the publisher, unless you didn't want to deal with the production and distribution of whatever version on your own (appears in all contracts).

"Ebook Reader Companies & Their Sales Outlets" may not

be acceptable to the author if the author has specific plans for marketing or selling the e-version of the books and the author has not already given the publisher exclusive e-rights (appears in the exclusive and non-exclusive ebooks contracts and the exclusive ebook & POD contract).

"Books on Demand Clause" may not be acceptable to an author who plans to personally handle print distribution or to sign with another POD or traditional print publisher. The author who agrees to this clause only agrees to let the publisher explore POD options on his behalf and the author has no other obligation (appears only in the exclusive and non-exclusive ebook contract).

"Short Run Printing Clause" allows the publisher to seek out short-term printing options without imposing any obligation on the author (appears in all contracts).

Paragraph 17 (a) means that any disputes with the publisher relating to the contract will be governed by the laws of the state in which the publisher is located (appears in all contracts).

ALEXA TRAFFIC RANK: 2,761,483

AUTHOR-FRIENDLY RATING: It's unclear from the publisher's web site what the author receives from publishing with the company. Without mention of services such as cover design, layout, or ISBN, there are too many loose ends.

I'm not thrilled with the calculation of "net revenue" because what's actually backed out from the retail price to calculate the royalty isn't well -defined. It's difficult to determine sales per book without knowing the costs. Also, the publisher's 10% holdback is not favorable.

The five-year contract length for all contracts, except the one-year exclusive ebook & POD contract, is too long. But because the author can terminate the contract with 10 days notice or with 90 days notice for the exclusive POD contract, the author-friendly rating remains relatively high.

I also found the web site amateurish and difficult to maneuver.

I suggest looking elsewhere for a publisher who clearly sets forth the author's costs and services rendered. There are simply too many holes in the information the publisher provides.

TRAFFORD PUBLISHING
www.trafford.com

FORMAT OF BOOK: POD and ebooks (included in some publishing packages).

PUBLISHING FEES: Offers three publishing packages (www.trafford.com/4dcgi/yourbookneeds.html):

Legacy Package $699 includes:

- ISBN
- LCCN
- Bar code
- Cover design and full-color cover
- 10 copies of author's paperback

The publisher only sells copies to the author and not to the general public.

Entrepreneur Package $999 includes:

- Every feature of the Legacy package (or equivalent upgrade below)
- Web page on publisher's web site
- Listing through publisher's online store
- 20 copies of author's book

Best Seller Package $1,399 includes:

- Every feature of the Entrepreneur package (or equivalent upgrade below)

- Submission to Amazon.com, Borders.com, Barnesand-Noble.com, Chapters.ca, Baker & Taylor, and Bowker's Books In Print
- Book made available for sale as an ebook
- Press release announcement to "thousands of book industry contacts"
- 40 paperback copies of author's book

ROYALTIES PAID TO AUTHOR: 60% of the "Gross Margin," which is the retail price less trade discount to booksellers and less the single copy printing cost.

The printing cost for a single copy of a 250-page book is $8.10, meaning that the minimum sale price has to be $20.25 (publisher allows author to set sale price, but it has to be at least 2.5 times more than the single copy cost (www.trafford.com/4dcgi/printing-costs-usa.html). Subtract Trafford's 25% trade discount (Trafford gives itself a trade discount for selling your books that you've paid to list on its web site) which is 25% of the retail price or $5.06. The $20.25 less the 25% Trafford discount of $5.06 and less the printing cost of $8.10, leaves a gross margin of $7.09 of which the author gets 60% or $4.25. Guess who gets the rest? The same company that already took 25% of the retail price.

If a book sells through Amazon.com, Amazon.com receives a 40% trade discount and Trafford doesn't take its 25% discount in this case. Once you've finished the math, you'll see that author's royalty on the $20.25 book sold through Amazon.com is approximately $2.43.

The royalty structure is detailed in Paragraph 11 of the Publishing Agreement at www.trafford.com/4dcgi/contract.html.

NOTABLE PROVISIONS OF THE PUBLISHING AGREEMENT: The publishing agreement can be found at www.trafford.com/4dcgi/contract.html.

Paragraph 14(1) confirms that the agreement is non-exclusive and that the author is free to publish with anyone else at any time.

Paragraph 14(2) allows either party to terminate at any time with written notice.

Paragraph 14(3) indicates that the contract is governed by the laws of British Columbia, Canada. Binding arbitration is the method to settle disputes, although the contract doesn't require arbitration to be physically held in British Columbia.

Paragraph 14(6) states that the author maintains all rights to the material at all times.

ALEXA TRAFFIC RANK: 63,149

AUTHOR-FRIENDLY RATING: In many respects, Trafford Publishing straddles the fence between the Just Okay and Publishers-To-Avoid categories. The sale prices of the books are outrageous. Unless the author sells copies to family and friends, it will be difficult to persuade average consumers to pay $20 or more for a 250-page book. Another problem is that Trafford double dips, which is my biggest publishing pet peeve. It takes a 25% bookseller discount, just as Amazon.com would, and then takes another 40% of the remainder. It earns an unjustifiably huge profit from printing the book. The cost to print a 250-page POD, standard paperback is about $4 at wholesale. These reasons alone are enough to dissuade me from considering them.

Moreover, its publishing fees are high for what you receive. The services provided in the Best Seller Package, which costs $1,399, can be found elsewhere for $800 to $1,000. Trafford charges $999 to make the book available for sale on its web site, whereas other publishers charge this basic service for $300 to $500.

The contract is the publisher's one bright spot. Terms are open and the contract is easy to terminate. Unfortunately, this alone isn't enough.

Why not include Trafford in Publishers-To-Avoid? Trafford remains a legitimate company. Many authors consider this publisher. While I wouldn't recommend it to anyone due to the retailing pricing, book printing costs, and royalty structure, you still receive the services you paid for.

This company places conspicuous advertisements in major writing magazine. It makes a ton of money off writers from the get-go, and a bunch more on the backside, if a writer is lucky enough to sell any books.

Although Trafford has devised a great business strategy, it would be a poor business decision for an author to choose this company.

UNIVERSAL PUBLISHERS
(formerly upublish.com)
www.universal-publishers.com

FORMAT OF BOOK: paperback and ebook

GENRES ACCEPTED: nonfiction only (mainly how-to, technical, and academic works)

PUBLISHING FEES: $495 ($395 if manuscript submission is in PDF format). The fee includes:
- ISBN
- Formatting for POD printing
- Conversion to PDF format (if not submitted as one);
- Web page on the publisher's web site for sales;
- Generic cover (custom covers cost an additional $100)

ROYALTIES PAID TO AUTHOR:

40% of the retail price for book sold on Universal Publishers

20% of the retail price for book sold through any third party

PRICE OF THE BOOK: All ebooks are $9. Paperbacks up to 200 pages sell for $19.95; 201- to 300-page paperback sells for $25.95; and 301- to 400-page paperback sells for $29.95.

NOTABLE PROVISIONS OF THE PUBLISHING AGREEMENT: The agreement can be found at www.universal-publishers.com/agreement.php.

The agreement is short: only three-fourths of a page. The third paragraph is the most important. It states that the contract is non-exclusive and can be canceled by either party with 90 days written notice. Two things to note: (1) if the publisher decides to terminate, the publishing fees paid by the author are nonrefundable, regardless of when the termination occurs, and (2) the publisher reserves the right to make the author repay all fees if author submits changes to the manuscript after it's been accepted for publication. In other words, if the book is ready to go and author discovers an error that must be changed, the publisher could make author pay additional $495.

ALEXA TRAFFIC RANK: 1,001,235

AUTHOR-FRIENDLY RATING: The contract is non-exclusive and easy to terminate. The set-up fee is reasonable. For $495, what you get is your book set up to be printed as a paperback and a page on the publisher's web site where the book will be offered for sale. That isn't much.

The royalty amounts are generous. The $9 price for ebooks makes sense, but the $19.95 cost for a 250-page book is high considering fledgling authors have few loyal followers willing to pay the price. That alone makes this publisher one of last resort.

WE PUBLISH
www.we-publish.com

FORMAT OF BOOK: print only

GENRES ACCEPTED: All, subject to approval

PUBLISHING FEES: $498 for a 50- to 300-page book (www.we-publish.com/pkginclude.htm), which includes:

- 5 free copies of your book
- Full color customized cover (not original artwork though)
- ISBN
- Listing in Bowker's Books In Print

ROYALTIES PAID TO AUTHOR:

30% of the retail price for books sold through publisher's web site

20% of the retail price for books sold through Amazon.com

SELLING PRICE OF YOUR BOOK: Determined by the publisher based on the number of pages and trim size. For details, see http://www.we publish.com/sellingprices.htm . A 250-page book with a 5.5" x 8.5" trim size retails for $16.95.

ROYALTIES PAID TO AUTHOR: 30% of the selling price for all books sold on the publisher's bookstore, www.1stbookstore. com. At $5.09, author receives an excellent royalty.

NOTABLE PROVISIONS OF THE PUBLISHING AGREEMENT: The entire publishing agreement is at www.we-publish.com/1wepubagreement.htm. This agreement has the potential to be very author-friendly, but the way it is currently written causes some concern.

There are two sections which discuss the publisher and author's obligations.

Under the section "We-publish.com/1stbookstore.com agrees to. . . .", the following paragraphs are important:

- Paragraph 7 gives the author an ebook version of the book which the author can sell or give away.

- Paragraph 9 is problematic: it says that all work will be sold for one year on the publisher's web site and will remain for sale each year thereafter so long as there are at least 10 sales a year. There is no finite term or even one that continues until either party terminates. The contract may be non-exclusive (Paragraph 2 under the section "Registered authors agree to the following. . . .") and the author can do whatever he wants with the book, BUT, conceivably, an author could be signed by Random House, and We Publish could continue to sell the book indefinitely.

OTHER SERVICES: A Marketing Services Package is offered for $1,295, which if the author can afford it, can be used to help boost sales. Since author can sell books elsewhere, the publicity from the Marketing Services Package could boost sales of the ebook form or even the print version sold through your own web site. You could do everything they do for $1,295, but it might take a while. The full marketing plan is at http://www.we-publish.com/marketing.htm.

Highlights include:

- Sending an ebook version for review to unlimited numbers of reviewers
- Sending four print books to reviewers
- Sending 100 press releases to appropriate media outlets
- Soliciting interview opportunities on as many as 12 local TV or radio stations
- Soliciting up to 15 book reviews and then providing those reviews to as many as 200 media outlets
- Posting on several book review web sites
- Soliciting and publicizing as many book signings according to author's preference

ALEXA TRAFFIC RANK: 1,008,162

AUTHOR-FRIENDLY RATING: The publishing contract is acceptable so long as the author limits its term. A preferable limit is one year, with automatic one-year renewal periods that either party can terminate with 30 days written notice.

The publishing fees and royalties are fine.

The web site is cumbersome, busy, and hard to use. While this publisher's services are in line with others, there wasn't much else to excite me.

WINGS PRESS

www.wings-press.com/guideline.htm

FORMAT OF BOOKS: ebooks and paperback

GENRES ACCEPTED:

A. Romance Novels in these subgenres:

- contemporary (50,000–150,000 words)
- historical (50,000–150,000 words)
- futuristic (50,000–150,000 words)
- fantasy (50,000–150,000 words)
- paranormal (50,000–150,000 words)
- sci-fi (romance must be a major part of the story; 50,000–150,000 words)
- romantic suspense (75,000–150,000 words)
- mystery romance (romance must be more than 50% of the story up to 150,000 words)
- mystery (cozy) (60,000–75,000 words)
- gothic (65,000–75,000 words)

B. Any genre with an older heroine (age 40 and above)

C. Young Adult (35,000 words minimum)

D. Middle Reader

E. General Fiction (75,000–150,000 words with little or no romance)

- mainstream
- historical
- adventure
- suspense
- espionage
- thriller
- light horror
- science fiction
- fantasy
- paranormal

PUBLISHING FEES: $0 for ebooks; $90 for POD

ROYALTIES PAID TO THE AUTHOR: 30% of the download price on ebooks. Ebooks sell for $6, so the author receives $1.80 per book.

For print books sold through the publisher's web site, the author receives $1.80 per book regardless of the book's retail price.

30% of the amount the publisher receives from the third party retailer for sales through third party retailers (according to information provided by the publisher's president, Lorraine Stephens).

NOTABLE PROVISIONS OF THE PUBLISHING AGREEMENT: President Lorraine Stephens informed me that the company doesn't provide samples of the contract, but did state that the contract is a two-year exclusive contract with one-year renewal periods.

According to Stephens, an author could terminate the contract at anytime (however, that's not what it says in the contract). Regardless of what any publisher tells you, if it's not in the contract, it's not enforceable. Period.

ALEXA TRAFFIC RANK: 1,208,451

AUTHOR-FRIENDLY RATING: A two-year exclusive contract is acceptable because the author pays few up-front fees. Remember, just because the publisher says an author can terminate at any time, it may be difficult to exercise this right if it's not in writing and in the publishing contract. Business contracts don't work that way. It's more likely the publisher will enforce contract terms and disregard anything outside its contract.

The $1.80 royalty for each POD book sale isn't favorable, especially for authors with long works. A 300-page book sells for about $12. The cost to print a 300-page book is about $4.80. Of the $7.20 that remains, the author receives $1.80 and the publisher makes $5.40. Under this calculation, the author only makes a 15% royalty.

While I have no reason to question Wings Press's intentions, I would stay away from any publisher that refuses to provide a sample contract. Without the benefit of examining the contract, I can only imagine how author-unfriendly its terms must be. Proceed with caution.

XLIBRIS.COM
www.xlibris.com

FORMAT OF BOOKS: POD

GENRES ACCEPTED: children's picture books and any other genre of fiction and nonfiction. Author pays publishing costs, so Xlibris is not selective.

PUBLISHING FEES: The publisher offers three packages: **Basic Service** $500 (www.xlibris.com/pubservices/ps_Basic. asp) includes:

- Generic cover
- ISBN and UPC bar code
- Registration with Amazon.com, Borders.com, Barnesand-Noble.com, Ingram, Books In Print, and more than 200 other online stores

Professional Service $900 (www.xlibris.com/pubservices/ps_professional.asp) includes:

- Everything in the Basic Service (or equivalent upgrade below), plus
- Book available as a hardback
- More choices of cover templates
- Registration with the U.S. Copyright Office
- LCCN

Custom Service $1,600 (www.xlibris.com/pubservices/ps_Custom.asp) includes:

- Everything in the Professional Service (or equivalent upgrade below), plus
- Custom-designed cover
- 10 hardback and 10 paperback copies of your book for your personal use or sale
- Premium placement on Xlibris web site

SELLING PRICES OF YOUR BOOKS: The prices of paperback and hardcover books depend on the number of pages and whether the book is sold through Xlibris or a reseller or distributor such as Amazon.com.

A 200- to 299-page paperback retails for $18.69 on Xlibris and $21.99 through Amazon.com. For a complete breakdown of the selling prices of the books in the various print formats and page numbers, go to http://www1.xlibris.com/bookpricing/chart2.pdf.

ROYALTIES PAID TO AUTHOR: Paperback and hardcover royalties are 10% of the retail price sold through a bookseller and 25% of the retail price sold through Xlibris.

NOTABLE PROVISIONS OF THE PUBLISHING AGREEMENT: The publishing agreement can be found at www. xlibris.com/pubservices/ps_author_agreement.asp.

"Your Work...Your Rights" states that Xlibris acquires no rights in the work and only provides services such as printing and book sales. The book will be printed the way the author submits it. Xlibris has no obligation to review or correct the work.

"Term & Exclusivity" states the contract is non-exclusive and the author can enter into other publishing agreements. If the author terminates the agreement during the first 30 days following publication, all publishing fees will be refunded in full. If Xlibris terminates at any time all publishing fees will be returned. Publishing fees are those fees directly associated with online, disk, and paper manuscript submission.

Under the section "Law and Venue" the parties agree to arbitrate disputes. Should either party want equitable relief or need to enforce the arbitrator's judgment, the remedy must be found in Pennsylvania. But, because of the way this section is written, should the author commence an arbitration proceeding, he may not necessarily be precluded from doing so in his own state.

ALEXA TRAFFIC RANK: 59,928

AUTHOR-FRIENDLY RATING: The contract itself is author-friendly enough.

What kills Xlibris are the publishing fees, the retail prices of the books, and the author price for copies. To get a customized book cover and copies of the book, the author must spend $1,600. You can find comparable services elsewhere for under $1,000.

The retail price of the books is also too high. This publisher sells a 230-page book through its own web site for $18.69, which is $4 to $5 more than what is reasonable. If the book sells through Amazon.com or another third party retailer, the price increases to $21.99. Who will pay that much for your book? Few consumers. Xlibris pays approximately $3.89 to print each 230-page paperback, and perhaps even less given their print volume. Look at the royalties again. For a 230-page paperback sold through Xlibris's web site, the author makes $5.50. Xlibris makes $9.30. If you don't have a problem with this uneven distribution, then consider this publisher.

The third negative about Xlibris is the price at which author's can purchase copies of their own books for resale That 230-page paperback can be purchased by the author for $13.19, a full $9.30 more than what it costs to print. If you purchase it for $13.19 (make sure you add in postage), you'll need to sell it for $20 to make any money. With this pricing structure, your book will have trouble competing in the marketplace.

Yes, this company mails one of the biggest, glossiest, high-quality brochures to *Writer's Digest* subscribers and other magazines. It's also partially owned by Random House. But if your priority is to sell books without paying an arm and a leg, forgo the glitz, save money, and move on to the next publisher.

CHAPTER 9

PUBLISHERS TO AVOID

If you choose to publish with any of the companies listed here, picture me whispering in your ear, "I told you so." It is harder to make the Publishers-to-Avoid list than it is to make the Outstanding list because I am not in the business of ruining people's livelihoods. I spent the most time trying to get these publishers to answer my questions, provide copies of their contracts, and explain why they do what they do.

Any publisher that refused to provide me a copy of their publishing contract ended up on this list (except Wings Press because the owner provided detailed information about the contract to me). If they don't want me to see it, there must be a good reason. Perhaps there's something in it that's not author-friendly and they assume by not providing a copy, the bad contract terms will never be discovered..

Other publishers ended up on this list because contract clauses were absolutely horrible. Some clauses required authors to give up rights for many years, to give up their ancillary rights to movies and TV, or engaged in other unsavory practices.

If the only publisher who will take your work is in this category, it's time for you to consider if writing is right for you.

I have no vendetta against these companies. I don't personally know anyone involved with them. I know how important your book is to you and my goal is to assist you in having a positive publishing experience. If you want to increase your chances of having a positive experience, go with one of the publishers described elsewhere in this book.

AUTHORHOUSE
www.authorhouse.com

FORMAT OF BOOK: ebook and paperback

GENRES ACCEPTED: All

PUBLISHING FEES:

Standard Paperback Publishing $698 includes:

- Full color cover design,
- ISBN
- Registration with online retailers

Additional $100 to publish as an ebook.

Color Paperback Option for $999 and requires the author to purchase 20 copies of the book. A description of their services can be found at http://www.authorhouse.com/GetPublished/ProductsServices.asp.

AuthorHouse offers optional services and fees for copyright registration, marketing and promotion packages, domain name registration, and more.

ROYALTIES PAID TO AUTHOR:

Ebooks: 25% of the purchase price

Print: royalty is based on the payment percentage selected by the author from the Book Pricing Agreement, which the author receives only after signing the contract and paying fee, and which is described below.

For a 230-page, 6"x 9" paperback on the publisher's web site, the author makes the corresponding royalty based on the prices listed below.

Price of Book	Royalty Amount
$9.90	5%
$10.40	10%
$11.00	15%
$11.70	20%
$13.40	30%
$18.70	50%

For books sold through third party retailers, the break down is as follows:

Price of Book	Royalty Amount
$14.49	5%
$15.99	10%
$18.49	15%
$21.49	20%

PRICE THAT AUTHOR PAYS FOR COPIES OF BOOK:

The author's price for a copy of the book is high.

To buy 99 or fewer copies of your paperback (230-page, 6"x9", standard paperback) it costs $9.71 per book, which includes shipping, even though the publisher pays less than $3.89 to print the book.

For orders of more than 100, the cost is $8.88 per book.

For orders of more than 250, the cost is $8.49 per book.

This publisher doesn't offer a substantial price break for such orders, especially when its cost per book progressively decreases.

NOTABLE PROVISIONS OF THE PUBLISHING AGREEMENT: A copy of the contract can be downloaded at http://www.authorhouse.com/GetPublished/Agreements.asp.

The precursor to this contract was horrible, and this dressed-up version shows little improvement. A few terms, such as the author's termination rights, have become more author-friendly, but others, such as remedies against the publisher, have worsened.

Here are some highlights (or lowlights) of the contract:

Sections 1.3 and 1.5 make it clear that the author will not receive the production files (the book cover, layout, etc.) from the publisher upon termination.

Section 1.6 gives AuthorHouse 180 days from the date on which it receives your work to have your work published.

Section 1.7 waives the author's channel access fees for the first year, but then charges those fees for all subsequent years.

Section 1.8 makes it clear that AuthorHouse provides no promotional assistance, unless the author purchases those additional services.

Section 5.6 is particularly troubling. AuthorHouse will not allow the author to transfer ownership interest or royalty rights to someone else without the express, written permission of AuthorHouse, which can be withheld at its "sole discretion for any reason." Given the rash of threatened and actual litigation against AuthorHouse, my guess is that this clause exists to prevent disgruntled authors from transferring their rights, including the right to sue, to a third party who may attempt to sue AuthorHouse.

The drafter of this contract seemed to anticipate author lawsuits and to prevent the types of suits and claims authors were making. Section 6.1 limits the author's remedy to having AuthorHouse either fix the problem ("use commercially reasonable efforts to cure") or to return the author's fees for the service at issue. Any author claim must be made within 30 days of the problem occurring. An author who is ready to make a claim or threatens legal action probably wants to get his money back and walk away from the publisher. My guess is that in 99% of the cases, AuthorHouse will "fix" the issue instead of refunding you a dime. If you plan on signing a contract with AuthorHouse, reread this paragraph many times.

Section 7.2 is the bright spot in an otherwise dismal contract. It allows the author to terminate the contract with 30 days written notice. The author, however, won't be entitled to a money refund.

Even if you are unhappy, the most you can ever get back is what you paid for the services. You can't receive lost profits or damages for pain and suffering.(covered in Section 4, the "Disclaimer"). The author who decides to sue, however, must file the claim for arbitration in AuthorHouse's hometown, Bloomington, Indiana. If AuthorHouse prevails, the author will be stuck paying AuthorHouse's legal fees.

ALEXA TRAFFIC RANK: 33,792

AUTHOR-FRIENDLY RATING: The best thing about AuthorHouse is the retail price for books sold through its web site and the corresponding author royalties.

The publishing fee is excessive for what you get, since all other services are à la carte. Those additional services are more expensive than most other PODs.. A review of prices for optional services reveals that the bulk of AuthorHouse's profits come off of its authors' backs and not from book sales. AuthorHouse charges $150 for copyright registration, while companies like www.click-andcopyright.com charge $97. AuthorHouse's copy editing services are $.015 per word, while many PODs charge $.01 per word, a 50% price difference.

Even more blatant is the $75 fee to register an author's domain name for one year. You can register your own domain name for one year for $8.50 at sites like www.dirt-cheap-domains.net. Finally, take a look at the Expanded Promotion option in Appendix B of the Publishing Agreement. What do you really get for $750? A press release that goes out to 500 media outlets (which is probably a general mass mailing); a book on how to market your book (that translates to, "We're not doing anything to help you"); review copies to the media if requested (it's up to you to get the media's attention); contacting you if the media requests an interview (again, you have to get the media interested); a book-signing kit (wouldn't you rather have them help you get book signings?); and the big catch-all that they will perform other activities that they deem appropriate (meaning they don't have to do a darn thing).

Further, any disagreement with AuthorHouse is a lost cause. Its contract makes it difficult to complain and see results. Even if you had a legitimate cause of action, it still might be impossible to win based on how the contract is written.

There is nothing favorable to the author. This company is for those authors who are willing to spend a ton of money to say their book is published. You'd be better off finding another publisher and taking your money and putting it towards marketing.

DENLINGER'S PUBLISHERS

www.thebookden.com

FORMAT OF BOOKS: ebooks and paperback (but rarely)

GENRES ACCEPTED: Anything except poetry, illustrated works, erotica, or text books. Manuscripts must be 100,000 words or less but more than 100 pages.

PUBLISHING FEES: $0

ROYALTIES PAID TO AUTHOR:

10% of all monies publisher receives from book sales

50% of all monies received from the sale of first serial rights, second serial rights, and movie rights

NOTABLE PROVISIONS OF THE PUBLISHING AGREEMENT: The contract is at www.thebookden.com/agree. html.

If you're thinking of going with this publisher, I'll save you a lot of trouble—DON'T! Here's why:

Paragraph 1 grants the publisher exclusive rights to publish the book in electronic and print formats during the term of the agreement. The contract doesn't specify the length of the term. Author also gives away additional rights, including the right to sell movie rights.

Between this and the pitiful 10% royalty, the contract only worsens.

Paragraph 5 gives the publisher the right of first refusal for the author's next two books in the same genre and under the same terms as the original book.

ALEXA TRAFFIC RANK: 3,020,520

AUTHOR-FRIENDLY RATING: P.T. Barnum once said, "There's a sucker born every minute." If you sign this contract, you'll be one of those suckers. This contract is an insult to the intelligence of any writer.

This is the only publishing contract in the epublishing or POD world that requires the writer's signature to be notarized. This is probably done to prevent authors, who later realize their mistake, from attempting to void the contract by claiming forged signatures or execution under duress.

HOLY FIRE PUBLISHING

www.christianpublish.com

FORMAT OF BOOKS: ebooks and POD

GENRES ACCEPTED: fiction, nonfiction, poetry, devotions, and youth books

PUBLISHING FEES: There are three packages available.

Plan A (Basic) $399 includes:

- 20% Author Royalty
- 35% Author Discount
- Basic formatting
- ISBN

Plan B (Premium) $699 includes everything in Plan A (or equivalent upgrade) plus:

- 30% Author Royalty
- 40% Author Discount
- 5 Free books

Plan C (Platinum): $1,299 includes everything in Plan B (or equivalent upgrade) plus:

- 30% Author Royalty
- 40% Author Discount
- 10 Free books
- Advanced Catalog Listing
- Custom Book Cover
- Ebook package
- 250 Postcards and Business Cards

An author without a cover design can create one through a template for $99 or get a custom one for $350. The publisher also charges $150 for ebook set -up and listing on Amazon.com.

Full explanation of the pricing is at http://www.christianpublish.com/price.htm.

Illustrations by an on-staff illustrator cost an additional $40 per page.

An advertisement in Ingram book distributor's catalog costs $119.

A typist can type your handwritten manuscript for $1.50 per page.

Postcards and business cards are available for $199–$299.

PRICE OF BOOKS: The retail price of the books depends on the page count (http://www.christianpublish.com/retailprice.htm). This is important since both the royalty and author's copies prices depend on the retail price. The author can purchase copies at either 35% or 40% off the retail price. A 230-page book retails for $14.99, so author copies cost from $8.99–$9.74. This price is close to the price at which authors can publish their books with other publishers. My biggest problem with this publisher and many others is that the publisher pays the printer, Lightning Source, about $3.89 per book. The publisher then marks up the price approximately 120% when it turns around and sells the book to the author.

ROYALTIES PAID TO AUTHOR: 20% of the wholesale price. Take a 230-page book which retails for $14.99. The wholesale price is $8.99, so you would make $1.80 per book. This isn't bad if someone is purchasing your book through Amazon.com. The shady part comes when someone purchases your book through Holy Fire. The retail price is still $14.99 and you still make $1.80 per sale. Holy Fire makes about $8 because it sells the book directly, and not through a distributor.

NOTABLE PROVISIONS OF THE PUBLISHING AGREEMENT: The entire contract can be found at http://www.

christianpublish.com/publishingagreement.pdf. In terms of author-friendliness, the contract is excellent. The author can terminate at any time with 60 days written notice. The only thing unclear here is that if you terminate, do you own the cover art and layout or formatting you paid to have created?

ALEXA TRAFFIC RANK: 4,106,497

AUTHOR-FRIENDLY RATING: Christian publishing is a booming business and there are many legitimate Christian publishers. Unfortunately, I can't in good conscience recommend this publisher to anyone. What bothers me most is when companies use religion to cover up rip-offs. On its homepage, Holy Fire tells authors, "You deserve a Publisher that only makes quality books and supports good Christian values." A publisher, which gives itself the same "trade discount" as Amazon.com and which pays authors the same royalty the author receives for Amazon.com sales, is scamming the author. I can't imagine any Christian values which fall under this pricing model.

The publisher also states, "We are one of the most reliable and affordable publishers in the industry because we consider this company a ministry." This really makes my blood boil. For $399, the author gets nothing except a book that is ready to be printed (assuming you have your own cover). This is just plain wrong. The $1,299 package is probably worth $600.

Yes, they have a great legal contract. But from a moral standpoint, this publisher should be ashamed of itself.

INKWATER PRESS
www.inkwaterpress.com

FORMAT OF BOOKS: POD paperbacks

GENRES ACCEPTED: All

PUBLISHING FEES: There are three packages for books with standard black-and-white interior (other packages for books with color interior):

Short Package $699 (www.inkwaterpress.com/pricing/pack_bwb.asp) for books up to 108 pages includes:

- Saddle stitching (staple binding), but additional $50 for perfect binding
- Listing at Amazon.com, BarnesandNoble.com, and Borders.com
- Submission to Books In Print
- Full color cover (from a template)
- ISBN and bar code
- 1 copy of book
- Author discounts of 40% to 55% of retail, depending on quantity ordered
- Royalties of 50% of the net receipts

Standard Package $899 (www.inkwaterpress.com/pricing/pack_bwi.asp) for books up to 700 pages includes everything in the Short Package (or equivalent upgrade) plus:

- Perfect binding
- Choice of book cover templates
- One-month free advertising on publisher's web site

Deluxe Package $1,299 (www.inkwaterpress.com/pricing/pack_bwd.asp) includes everything in the Standard Package (or equivalent upgrade) plus:

- Custom-designed cover
- 5 copies of your book
- More trim size choices

ROYALTIES PAID TO AUTHOR: 50% of the net receipts

NOTABLE PROVISIONS OF THE PUBLISHING AGREEMENT: Despite two e-mail requests for a sample contract, publisher failed to respond.

OTHER SERVICES OFFERED:

- Editing Services (www.inkwaterpress.com/services/editing.asp)

  Basic proofreading is $.025 per word, which is $.015 higher than many publishers.

  Light editing is $.03–$.05 per word, and includes proofreading and suggested corrections and comments on style.

  The editing services are higher than any other POD publisher I've seen. Before you select Inkwater's editing services, you may want to shop around.

- Marketing packages (www.inkwaterpress.com/pricing/pubfeatures.asp). Variety of packages are available depending on the type of book. Most involve media kit creation and delivery to parties who may be interested. For example, the $4,350 Trade Bookstores Mailing Package includes delivery of a full color sales sheet and targeted letter to 1,368 trade bookstores. Is this service beneficial? It's unclear whether the publisher targets appropriate stores or uses the same list for every customer and pays someone $6 an hour to stuff the envelopes. My guess is the latter.

This publisher also offers web site development packages. The $750 package includes preparation of five pages and a shopping cart, which is a reasonable set-up fee. The package does not include maintenance, which costs an additional $60 per hour (minimum of $30 per change request).

ALEXA TRAFFIC RANK: 1,442,371

AUTHOR-FRIENDLY RATING: Have you ever had a bad gut feeling? Inkwater Press invokes this feeling in me. The publishing packages are over-priced: a $699 package which doesn't include a customized cover and includes one complimentary copy is absurd. Add to that its blatant refusal to acknowledge my e-mail requests, and it spells trouble for you. Any publisher that delivers poor customer service to potential clients is one better avoided.

KISOL BOOKS
www.kisolbooks.com

FORMAT OF BOOKS: POD paperbacks

GENRES ACCEPTED: general fiction and non-fiction, children's books, educational books, technical and scientific books, religious and spiritual books

PUBLISHING FEES: $299 fee includes:
- Cover made with author's graphics and specification
- Layout and book formatting
- Standard paperback binding
- Authors can submit unlimited graphics
- ISBN
- Web page on the publisher's web site on which book is sold

PRICE OF BOOKS: The retail price of your book is determined by Kisol Books, which typically charges three to four times the cost to produce book.

ROYALTIES PAID TO AUTHOR: 20% of the royalties from sales of book

NOTABLE PROVISIONS OF THE PUBLISHING AGREEMENT: The contract can be found at http://www.kisol-books.com/agreement.pdf. There are several problems with this contract. Although "Royalties" states that the author receives a 20% royalty from sales of the book, the 20% is not defined. Are royalties 20% of the retail price or the net price? This clause is simply too open-ended.

Under normal circumstances, I would suggest that the vagueness of the royalty section is permissible because the provision would be construed in U.S. courts in the light most favorable to the non-drafting party, which is almost always the author. But "Law and Jurisdiction" provides that the laws of England and Wales govern. Any lawsuit must be heard in England or Wales.

While an author can terminate with only 30 days notice, under "Terms, Conditions and Exclusiveness," the publisher retains all "digital property and ownership related to all completed production data files." The rights to the cover and formatting stays with the publisher.

ALEXA TRAFFIC RANK: 3,196,564

AUTHOR-FRIENDLY RATING: For any U.S. author, this company makes no sense because it's based in South Africa. In fact, no writer anywhere should choose Kisol Books. For $299, the author receives little value. Perhaps the only value is the ISBN. Other services do not amount to much. A publisher that takes the author's rights to the cover art is not worth much.

In addition, the retail price of books is too high. This company's fees and services are simply a head shaker.

PAGEFREE PUBLISHING, INC.
www.pagefreepublishing.com

FORMAT OF BOOK: ebooks and POD paperbacks and hardbacks

GENRES ACCEPTED: All

PUBLISHING FEES: There are several pricing options for paperback and hardcover books. This review only covers paperback fees.

The pricing for paperback is based on word count:

Up to 70,000 words	$299
70,000–120,000 words	$349
120,000–150,000 words	$419

And includes:

- Customized full color cover (from stock art or provided by the author)
- ISBN
- Bar code
- Book made available through Ingram, internet retailers such as Amazon.com, and the publisher's online store (www.thegreatamericanbookstore.com)
- Listing with Bowker's Books In Print
- Additional $25 to make book available as an ebook

ROYALTIES PAID TO AUTHOR: 75% of the net profit per book sold. "Net Profit" is defined as the list price less the wholesale or trade discount and less the cost of printing. For details, see the "Accounting" section of the Publishing Agreement.

The publisher's schedule allows the author to calculate the

cost of printing the book in the various formats. A 5"x 8" or 6"x 9" 300-page paperback costs $6.60 to print ($1.20 per cover + $.018 per page). Because this cost applies to copies printed for sale through a third party retailer, the author must price the book higher than $14 to earn a profit. Amazon.com and other retailers take, at minimum, a 50% discount.

Here's the killer. PageFree Publishing gives itself the same discount it gives to Amazon.com. The publisher's explanation for taking the same discount is that "any books we order for fulfillment are sold to us at a higher price than those ordered by Ingram to fulfill bookstore orders. We are also charged an additional handling fee, as well as our own administrative/credit card costs."

Despite PageFree's attempt to justify its discount, taking the same discount as Amazon.com remains a shady practice and makes the 75% author royalty misleading. PageFree makes most of the money from the sale of a book, while making it appear as though the author receives most of the money. For example, take a book that sells for $15 on PageFree's online store. Assume the printing costs are $5. If you were really getting a 75% royalty, you'd receive $7.50 from the sale. But PageFree gives itself a 55% discount off the price of the book which equals $8.25. Subtract $5 in printing costs and the $8.25 discount from the $15 retail price and the author is left with 75% of a net profit of $1.75, which equals $1.31.

For author copies, the price per book is $1.80 plus $.022 per page, which is much higher than the publisher's actual printing cost. Publishers pay about $.90 per cover and $.013 per page. A 300-page, 5" x 8" paperback will cost an author $8.40 per book for a minimum order of 25 books, not including shipping charges. The cost at which you can purchase your books from this publisher is cheaper than most, but it's probably the only highlight.

NOTABLE PROVISIONS OF THE PUBLISHING AGREEMENT: The publishing agreement is at http://pagefreepublishing.com/PDFgallery.htm.

The first paragraph grants PageFree a non-exclusive license to sell the book in print or electronic formats during the term. In the middle of the third paragraph under "Accounting," the author can terminate the agreement at any time with 30 days written notice. The fourth paragraph under "Accounting" specifies Kalamazoo County, Michigan, or the Federal Court in the Western District of Michigan, as the venue for any legal dispute.

Although the contract is author-friendly, PageFree fails to approach its pricing structure with the same philosophy.

ADDITIONAL SERVICES: Editing, graphics, additional formats, and marketing services are available for an additional fee. The editing services seem to be a good deal. The price depends on the word count, but basic editing for a 70,001–120,000 words is $225. The services includes spelling, grammar, and sentence structure checks.

ALEXA TRAFFIC RANK: 2,433,952

AUTHOR-FRIENDLY RATING: Although publishing fees are in the right ballpark and the contract is author-friendly, the publisher discount is underhanded and outweighs the positives. PageFree is one of the few publishers I know of which applies this wholesale discount to sales from its web site. The 75% royalty amount, in actuality, is closer to 10% or 12% for books sold through the publisher's web site and third party online retailers like Amazon.com. I strongly disapprove of any publisher that gives itself a wholesale discount, and wouldn't recommend this publisher which takes money directly out of the author's pockets. There is nothing illegal about this practice, but it is misleading to persuade authors into thinking they receive 75% royalties when the truth is far from this case. If PageFree stopped this practice, they'd be ranked much higher.

PROTEA PUBLISHING

www.proteapublishing.com

FORMAT OF BOOKS: Paperback and hardcover

GENRES ACCEPTED: All

PUBLISHING FEES: Two publishing packages:

$390 flat fee, which includes

- Cover art,
- Sales page on the publisher's web site equipped with Paypal to accept orders

Free publishing, as long as:

- Author purchases minimum of 75 books at 60% of the retail price For example, if the retail price of the book is $15, then author pays $9 per book, or $675 for 75 books.

ROYALTIES PAID TO AUTHOR: 50% of the "Net Retail Price." Sounds great at first, but this is another publisher that gives itself a 40% retailer's discount. Take one of its web site books, *My Sugga Daddy Ain't So Sweet!*, as an example. This 160-page paperback retails for $15.90. The publisher pays $2.98 to print the book. It then takes a 40% discount, or $6.36, to sell the book. After subtracting the cost of printing and the publisher's discount fee, the author is left with a net retail price of $6.56. Subtract the publisher's additional $3.28, and the author makes only $3.28 for a book that retailed close to $16.

COST TO AUTHOR FOR BOOKS: Depends on how many you buy. You get a 40% discount off list on 75 copies or more; 30% discount off list on 50 copies or more; 20% discount off list on 25 copies or more. But this is a terrible deal for authors. An author who doesn't experience a big demand for books will be tying up money and sitting on inventory. If you need only a few copies, you won't make any money. Let's say you buy 25 books and receive 20% off a retail price of $15, or $12. By the time those books are shipped to you and you add in postage costs, you've paid close to the retail price. You'll spend $300 to buy 25 books that you thought you could sell for $375.

The publisher uses Lightning Source to print a book. Lightning Source's charge to the publisher to print one book via POD technology is the same as it is to print 100. So why does the publisher charge you more per book to purchase 25 copies than it does if you purchase 75 copies? Get it?

NOTABLE PROVISIONS OF THE PUBLISHING AGREEMENT: The publishing agreement can be found at http://www.proteapublishing.com/agreement.htm.

This contract is so poorly written that even a dimwitted lawyer should be able to get you out of it. But a contract that requires an author to engage a lawyer is not one you should consider.

"Author Retains Rights" gives the publisher rights to the cover art, which you paid for, if you want to publish the book elsewhere.

"Support" requires the author to communicate with Protea Publishing in writing. You are trusting your book Protea Publishing and you should be able to speak to the publisher whenever you want.

"Author's Exit Clause" is the most troubling contract provision. In Protea Publishing's previous contract, the author gave Protea the exclusive right to publish the book for the "length of the contract," which had no set term and could theoretically last forever. Its current contract allows you to terminate only if Protea fails to pay royalties for four consecutive quarters or to perform pursuant to the agreement. Protea can withhold royalties for a year, and when an author threatens to sue for royalties, it can pay up and avoid litigation. There's virtually no way out for the author.

The contract is non-exclusive, but Protea will always have the right to publish your book regardless of what you do.

ALEXA TRAFFIC RANK: 2,899,798

AUTHOR-FRIENDLY RATING: You'd be crazy to sign this contract, which is designed to allow Protea to make money at the expense of its authors. An author pays $390 up front and doesn't even retain ownership of the files containing the cover and layout. The publisher also pretends it's Amazon.com by taking 40% of your book price in exchange for selling it on its web site. It then takes another 50% from the remaining amount.

There's no way out of the contract unless Protea stiffs you on royalties for one year and then refuses to pay up.

Plus, do you want to sign a contract with a publishing company who misspells likelihood as "likely hood" in its contract and seems to forget that punctuation is essential to good writing? Save yourself some grief and misery: don't allow Protea to publish your work. If Protea is the only publisher willing to publish your work, then it's time to evaluate your talent as a writer, and not time to shell out money.

PUBLISHAMERICA

www.publishamerica.com

FORMAT OF BOOKS: paperback and ebooks

GENRES ACCEPTED: Fiction and non-fiction works that deal with challenges, real or imagined. Since most novels deal with overcoming personal challenges and hardships, Publish America considers most fiction. For non-fiction, the publisher is most interested in how-to guides, biographies, manuals, and history, religion, and health books.

PUBLISHING FEES: $0. PublishAmerica claims to operate like a traditional publisher, but it operates like a traditional publisher only in theory. The contract terms are so outrageous that except for not charging an up-front publishing fee, PublishAmerica and traditional publishers have nothing in common..

Graphic designers paid by the publisher create the cover art. Editors edit the books. The publisher registers the ISBN and obtains a bar code.

The author receives complimentary books and assistance with marketing efforts for a direct mail campaign. The publisher submits titles to wholesalers and distributors (Ingram, Baker & Taylor, Brodart) and the titles can be ordered by bookstores in North America.

ROYALTIES PAID TO AUTHOR:

8% on the first 2,000 copies sold,

10% on the next 8,000 copies sold, and

12.5% on all copies over 10,000.

It's unclear whether royalties are based on the book's wholesale or retail price.

NOTABLE PROVISIONS OF THE PUBLISHING AGREEMENT: This publisher won't provide a copy of the contract until it's accepted your work. I was lucky enough to get a contract from one of the many furious authors who've published with PublishAmerica.

After reading the contract, I know why this publisher doesn't want anyone to see it. The first clue that something shady might be going on is that the address listed for the company is a post office box.

There isn't one legitimate traditional publisher that would expect an author to sign a contract like PublishAmerica's.

Section 1 grants exclusive rights to publish the book in all formats for seven years worldwide to PublishAmerica. This seems reasonable at first glance because the publisher fronts all printing and publishing costs. But, a closer look at the contract language makes it clear what's really going on here.

Section 9 assigns to PublishAmerica all other print rights, such as translations, book club sales, motion picture, radio, serial, and television. Should the publisher sell any of those rights, the author receives only 50% of any monies earned. Traditional publishers don't operate like this.

Section 10 sets forth the price at which authors purchase copies from the publisher. The author receives a 20% discount of the retail price for orders fewer than 20. For orders of more than 20, the author receives a 30% discount, which is far less than almost every publisher rated in this book. The only bright spot of the contract is in this section: the author keeps all monies from sales the author makes from her copies. This bright spot is likely the result of the PublishAmerica's inability to monitor the author's sales.

Section 20 gives PublishAmerica the exclusive right to negotiate all movie, television, radio, and other rights on the author's behalf, and requires the author to approve the negotiations. It states, "Approval of all terms, provisions and conditions of any and all contracts in connection with any such sale, lease, license or other disposition **shall be given** by the Author . . . ."

One final slap in the author's face is that the prevailing party in a lawsuit is not awarded attorneys' fees. Normally, leaving this out would favor authors, but in this case, it's probable that the majority of lawsuits are brought by dissatisfied authors and not PublishAmerica.

ALEXA TRAFFIC RANK: 72,264

AUTHOR-FRIENDLY RATING: If the world of self-publishing has an Evil Empire, PublishAmerica occupies that role. One author who contacted me hired a lawyer and spent thousands of dollars to get out of her contract. She was more than willing to provide a copy of the contract and valuable information about the way PublishAmerica treats its authors. Shocking, disgusting, and despicable are just a few of the adjectives to describe this publisher's practices.

The respected Preditors & Editors web site, http://www.invir-tuo.cc/prededitors/pebp.htm, all but calls PublishAmerica a scam. The web site has links to related material about this publisher, including a story in the San Antonio Current (6/24/04) available at http://sacurrent.com/website/news.cfm?newsid=12073075&BRD=2318&PAG=461&dept_id=484045&rfi=6.

Also, Science Fiction and Fantasy Writer's of America's (www.SFWA.org) Writers Beware web site section devotes a whole page to the "PublishAmerica Hoax" at http://sfwa.org/beware/general.html#PA .

Consider yourself warned.

STONE DRAGON PRESS

www.stonedragonpress.com

FORMAT OF BOOKS: paperback

GENRES ACCEPTED: For an author without an agent, this publisher accepts: science fiction (hard or soft), speculative fiction, horror, fantasy (high or low), and science fantasy. For an author represented by an agent, the publisher accepts any fiction.

PUBLISHING FEES: $0
ROYALTIES PAID TO THE AUTHOR: 10% of the cover price

NOTABLE PROVISIONS OF THE PUBLISHING AGREEMENT: The contract is at www.stonedragonpress.com/sub_contract.html. This is the lengthiest POD contract I've ever seen.

Section 1 grants to Stone Dragon Press the exclusive paperback rights in English for five years. Ebook rights are specifically excluded. Section 1(5) doesn't allow for a clean break after the five-year term expires because the publisher has 60 days to negotiate a new deal with the author. If no agreement can be reached, the publisher retains its current rights (exclusive paperback) until the author sends written notification. After the author's notification, the publisher still retains those rights for an additional 90 days.

The publisher buys itself another six months while the book remains in limbo. This may prove troublesome for an author who is about to sign with another publisher.

Section 2 representations and warranties are standard and reasonable.

Section 3 "Manuscript and Delivery" is standard. Stone Dragon Press uses a lot of words to say, You have to give us the book on disk in a form we can read...If you need authorizations from third parties you have to furnish them...You also need to file the copyright for your book...If you don't do these things, we can do them for you and charge you.

Section 3, Subsection 4 is somewhat troublesome. It appears that if the publisher determines that your book needs editing, it can edit it and charge you for it. The publisher wants to operate like a traditional publisher, but this editing charge throws them a step back. Any author considering this publisher should have this section clarified or removed, or risk facing a hefty editing bill.

Section 4 "Publication" is an example of a publisher adopting the traditional publisher's practice: it gives itself one year to deliver your book to market. A typical POD publisher takes 90 to 180 days to publish a book.

Section 5 "Cover Art" explains the process of selecting the cover artist. It gives the author a lot of say over the book cover design.

Section 5 "Interior Illustrations" also gives the author control over book illustrations.

Section 7(a) specifies that Stone Dragon Press will register the copyright for the author. The publisher also has the right to commence a lawsuit and any monies recovered from an infringement lawsuit will be divided between the author and the publisher.

Section 9(2) may confuse the author. I can't figure out where the "original cost of composition" came from. Ask the publisher for a clear explanation of this section.

Section 10 is where this contract begins to unravel. During the five-year term, the author cannot publish anything that directly competes with the work. What does that mean? If you publish a novel about aliens attacking earth with Stone Dragon, and subsequently publish a new novel about different aliens attacking the earth, is this new novel considered directly competitive? Don't consider signing a contract with this restrictive clause, especially with a publisher that has no major distribution.

Subsection 10(2) states that the author can license all reserved rights under the agreement to anyone. Section 13 describes the publisher's subsidiary rights and Section 16 describes the author's reserved rights (film/TV, merchandising, and more).

Section 11 "Royalties & License" matches a traditional publisher's royalties. But while the royalties are on par with traditional publishers, they remain quite low for POD publishers. In addition, the publisher can reserve up to 35% of the author's royalties to cover any returns from booksellers.

Section 13 grants the publisher the following rights: first and second serial rights, book club rights and reprint rights (into other languages). The author receives 50% of any such sale of rights.

Section 20 "Reversion & Termination" describes all situations that trigger contract termination, such as voluntary cancellation by the publisher after two years. The author has no way to proactively terminate the contract before the expiration of the five-year term but, instead, remains dependent on the publisher's discontinuation of the work, failure to print, failure to pay royalties, and bankruptcy (discussed fully in Section 21 "Bankruptcy & Insolvency").

Section 23 requires the publisher and author to arbitrate disputes in St. Paul, Minnesota, except in cases where the publisher fails to pay royalties. In that case, the author can sue in court instead of resorting to arbitration.

Section 26 requires the publisher to execute any required documents to memorialize the transfer of rights if the rights in the author's book revert back to the author before the end of the five-year term. The documents clarify that Stone Dragon no longer has any claim to any rights in the book.

Section 28 means that if the author, Stone Dragon, or both, assign rights to the publishing agreement to other parties, those new parties are bound by the terms of the contract. In addition, Section 22 says that no assignment is binding on either party without written consent of the other (except in cases where the author wants to assign his royalties to a third party).

ALEXA TRAFFIC RANK: 4,108,495

AUTHOR-FRIENDLY RATING: Yes, there's no publishing fee. But Stone Dragon Press is hardly a traditional publisher. They have few writers and no distribution. Its books can only be purchased through Amazon.com or from another web site associated with Stone Dragon. If Bantam came to you with this contract, I'd tell you to sign it, because Bantam is a major publisher. But Stone Dragon is not Bantam. You'd be crazy to sign over your publishing rights to Stone Dragon Press for five years.

Unless and until I hear that Stone Dragon Press is causing a stir in the publishing world, I would not publish my book with them. Look for a publisher that won't demand exclusive print rights for more than one year.

UNLIMITED PUBLISHING

www.unlimitedpublishing.com

FORMAT OF BOOK: POD (hard cover & paperback)

GENRES ACCEPTED: All

PUBLISHING FEES: $500, but requires an additional $1,000 to cover book design and layout. The real cost of publishing with Unlimited Publishing is approximately $1,500 (not including an additional 25% for hardcover).

This fee includes:

- ISBN
- Book cover
- 100 press releases sent to newspapers, magazines, radio and TV stations
- Announcement of the book on various Internet locations
- Author's web page on publisher's web site

ROYALTIES PAID TO AUTHOR: 50% of the Net Proceeds as detailed at www.unlimitedpublishing.com/income.htm. Read the provision on the web site carefully and do the math. You end up receiving 10% of the cover price for sales through the publisher's web site. You receive $1.50 per book for sales through third party retailers. Authors have the option to order copies at cost and to sell them on their own. Personal sales could yield a royalty of between $4 and $7.50 per book.

NOTABLE PROVISIONS OF THE PUBLISHING AGREEMENT: The publishing agreement can be found at www. unlimitedpublishing.com/8subform.htm.

The third paragraph grants the publisher "the exclusive right to reproduce the work in any form for a period of one year following publication." In addition to print, the publisher can sell and distribute your book in any format. The fees pay for preparation of the print book only, but the contract requires you to give the publisher all electronic rights.

Lines 1 through 8 below the third paragraph are standard. But line 9 is where things become unfavorable for the author. It's reasonable for an author to be liable to the publisher in cases where, for example, the publisher is sued for copyright infringement because the author lied to the publisher about the author's ownership of the work, or for any other reason listed in lines 1 through 8.

But line 9 indicates that the author must pay all publisher's legal expenses as a result of its entering into the agreement. The intent here may have been that in a situation where the publisher is sued because of the author's violation of lines 1 through 8, the author has to reimburse the publisher for legal expenses it incurred in defending itself against a third party. However, this language is too broad and could be interpreted to require the author to pay the publisher's legal expenses in a dispute between the author and publisher, even if the author ultimately prevailed.

An author signing the contract should request modification to line 9 as follows:

> ". . .including legal expenses, that UP may incur
> as a result of legal actions against it by third parties
> due to UP's entering into this Agreement with the
> contributor."

This modified language makes it clear that the author will never have to pay UP's legal expenses for a dispute between the author and the publisher (UP).

Next, go to the portion of the agreement where it reads, "In consideration of this AGREEMENT, UP SHALL: . . ." and look at paragraph 8. Paragraph 8 makes it clear that all editing work is the author's responsibility. For $1,500, you'd think the publisher would be willing to correct a few errors.

Paragraph 10 permits the publisher to terminate the agreement at any time. Theoretically, they could take your publishing fee, terminate the agreement, and not return any portion of the fee you paid. I have no reason to believe this would happen, nor have I heard of this publisher carrying out this practice since it would be fraudulent and would subject them to criminal prosecution. But on its face, the contract terms allows it and there is no part of this agreement that details what portion of the publishing fee the publisher would return to the author if the agreement was published prior to publication. Many PODs that have termination language similar to this specifically state that the publishing fee will be returned if the publisher terminates the agreement prior to publication.

Next, go to the portion of the agreement that starts with, "In consideration of this AGREEMENT, the CONTRIBUTOR shall: . . . ." Paragraph 1 under this section explains that the author must provide the publisher 60 days written notice before the author can terminate the contract. The contract will continue on after the first year until the author gives notice to terminate.

No author should sign the publisher's contract without having Paragraphs 7 and 8 removed. Paragraph 7 gives the publisher up to 50% of the author's rights in the work during the term of this agreement. This grant excludes the right to any monies the author earns from sales of the copies the author purchased from the publisher. Your book's success depends on your efforts. If you are fortunate to find someone who offers to buy the movie, television, or other rights during the term of the contract, the publishing company as the holder of 50% of those rights will benefit or even hinder your efforts. Any deal you try to make will require the publishing company's approval as the 50% owner of the rights. What has this publisher done to deserve a 50% stake in all the rights to your work? Very little.

Paragraph 8 is nothing short of despicable. For one year following the termination of the agreement, the publisher retains a 10% interest in all the author's rights to the work. If you terminate the agreement because Random House offered you a contract for which you will receive a $10,000 advance, guess who receives $1000 of it? The publisher does not deserve this windfall that resulted from your efforts.

Paragraph 9 also contains offensive language. It requires the author to "prominently" list the publisher's name and URL in any announcement the author sends out relating to the book. The publisher encourages you to purchase copies at wholesale and sell them on your own, so why should you have to waste any space promoting them? Your job is to promote your work, not their business.

Notice also that should a dispute arise between you and the publisher, it must be resolved in Boston, Massachusetts, or wherever the company chooses. And regardless of the dispute, the publisher is not responsible for any amount more than the publishing fees the author paid. Requiring the author to travel to Boston and limiting the publisher's responsibility to the publishing fee amount is a sure way to discourage and deter any author from filing a lawsuit.

ALEXA TRAFFIC RANK: 1,971,233

AUTHOR-FRIENDLY RATING: The author pays an outrageous fee, $1,500 or more, to get the book in POD format. The 50% royalty sounds great, until you discover you'll only receive about 10% of the cover price. The only bright spot is that the publisher allows authors to buy copies of their book for resale for about 50% of the cover price, thus making it possible for authors to earn an acceptable royalty for books they sell themselves.

But this positive aspect disappears once the publisher crushes you with high prices and terrible contract terms. It shamelessly hijacks your rights. Stay away.

YOUR BOOK PUBLISHER
www.yourbookpublisher.com

FORMAT OF BOOKS: POD

GENRES ACCEPTED: All

PUBLISHING FEES: Current fees not available. Fees are not listed on its web site and the publisher refused to provide this information upon request.

The fees below are from publishing packages offered in 2004:

Production Plan costs $3.50 per final book page (250-page book costs $875), and includes:

- Full-color laminated cover
- ISBN number and barcode
- Copyright registration
- Listing on the publisher's web site
- Listing on Amazon.com, BarnesandNoble.com, and Borders.com.

Custom Plan includes all of the elements of the Production Plan, and offers additional services such as editing.

RETAIL PRICE OF THE BOOK: One of the questions the publisher did answer was this one. The retail price of a 230-page paperback is $19 to $21. This is extremely high and should be between $12 and $14.

ROYALTIES PAID TO THE AUTHOR: 15% of the list price

NOTABLE PROVISIONS OF THE PUBLISHING AGREEMENT: There is no contract available on the web site. The publisher did send me a copy, and allowed me to "paraphrase its content without conveying the legalistic terminology."

Sounds like a threat, doesn't it? I, of course, will respect the wishes of the publisher.

Section 2 states that it is non-exclusive.

Section 4(d) states that the author can purchase copies (10 or more) for a price equal to 50% of the book's list price, plus shipping. Since the list price is so high, the 50% purchase price for authors is a terrible deal. Like most POD publishers, this publisher uses Lightning Source to print books. A 230-page paperback (with full color cover) costs the publisher $3.89 to print. If it retails the book for $20, the author pays $10, giving the publisher a $6.11 profit. It's good to be a publisher isn't it? After shipping costs, the author has now paid $10.50. A 230-page book, to be competitive, can only sell for about $12 to $14, leaving the author with a pittance.

Section 6 requires binding arbitration. The contract doesn't specify the venue for arbitration proceedings and hearings. This means that the author may attempt to arbitrate a dispute in his hometown, and not in the publisher's backyard.

Section 10 allows either party to terminate the contract at any time. After termination, the publisher can continue to sell your book for up to one year. If you consider signing with this publisher insist on removing language giving the publisher this right.

ALEXA TRAFFIC RANK: No data

AUTHOR-FRIENDLY RATING: The publisher's web site now says it publishes most authors for free. I'm not sure this isn't a bait-n-switch technique. I find it hard to believe that Your Book Publisher went from charging $3.50 per page to publishing the book for free.

What scares me even more is the contract clause that permits the publisher to continue selling your book after contract termination. This provision ruins an otherwise fair contract. There's little reason to sign this publisher's contract.

CONCLUSION

You Found a Publisher, Now What?

If you follow the advice in this book, you'll more than likely end up with a great publisher and an author-friendly contract. But, no matter how reputable your publisher is or how favorable your contract terms turn out, these factors are nothing more than the birthing center for your book . Ultimately you want to be in a position to either be your own publisher or sign a lucrative contract with a traditional publisher. The great thing about the good publishers in this book is that they can put you in a position to control your publishing destiny. If your book really starts selling, pull it from the publisher, start your own publishing company, and keep all the profits. Of course, if your book really does start selling, you'll also receive interest from traditional publishers seeking you out. The key is learning how to effectively market your book.

Your book's success will depend entirely on you. In today's publishing world, the first-time novelist fortunate enough to sign a contract with Random House and the first-time author who pays one of the publishers listed in this book, launch off in the same boat. Sure, the other guy brags to his friends about his "publishing deal," but that's where the difference ends. Virtually all traditional publishers expect new authors to market and promote their own books with little or no monetary assistance. They face the same uphill marketing battle that as a self-publishing author like you faces.

If you can't afford a book publicist like BookPros, you'll have to dive in and do it yourself. One affordable place to find good resources to market your book is at www.book-marketing-tools. com. For $15, you get links and contact information for numerous web sites on which you can post information about your new release. You'll also receive contact information for book reviewers who will review books by emerging writers like you.

If you are just seeking some great self-publishing resources, visit www.go-publish-yourself.com, which, in both 2004 and 2005, *Writer's Digest* rated one of the best web sites for writers.

To market yourself and your book effectively, it's also essential to have a web site. Don't necessarily rely on the web page which your publisher provides. Your web site should play the role of more than an informational brochure. It should sell your book. Make sure it's set up for optimal search engine placement. Sell as many copies of your book as possible from your web site, and/or drive those visitors to your book's page on Amazon.com or similar sites, or both. Having a functional web site is a critical element in your success and this topic could be an entire book of its own. If you want to see an example of what I'm talking about, visit the web site for my new novel at www.saturn-return.com.

If your book covers a subject which other people will likely find through online searches, then purchase advertising on Yahoo (www.overture.com) and Google (www.adwords.google.com). For example, if your book is about dog grooming, then find out which popular terms people enter when searching for this topic (e.g. "dog grooming, pet grooming, etc.). Write up an engaging ad, get people to your web site, and sell books. Yes, it's not that simple, but it's incredibly effective and it works. The first version of *The Fine Print of Self-Publishing* was only in ebook form and exclusively advertised online as described above. It works.

If you would like to learn more about how to create a web site that will help you sell books and make online advertising work for you, e-mail me at Mark@ClickIndustries.com. My company operates 16 different web sites. Their success and effectiveness are the result of being perfectly optimized and advertised through, targeted, online advertising campaigns. It's how my company does business everyday. In fact, you probably found this book through online advertising.

Whatever you choose to do with your book, it's an accomplishment to have completed and published it. How many people do you know have a book inside of them, and yet never find the time or courage to write it?

I wish you success with your book. I hope I've helped make the process, especially your decision about publishing options, easier and less stressful. Good luck and good writing!

Printed in the United States
49681LVS00002B/133-510

9 781933 538563